Understa... Response to Intervention

A Practical Guide to Systemic Implementation

Robert Howell

Sandra Patton

Margaret Deiotte

Solution Tree

555 North Morton Street
Bloomington, IN 47404

(800) 733-6786 (toll free)
(812) 336-7700
FAX: (812) 336-7790

email: info@solution-tree.com
www.solution-tree.com

Cover design by Grannan Design, Ltd.

Printed in the United States of America

ISBN 978-1-934009-34-5

Acknowledgments

We appreciate the guidance and foresight of the Colorado Department of Education and the Colorado Springs School District 11 Board of Education. Their leadership in establishing RTI as a state and district priority provided our impetus for seeing RTI in the light of systemic change.

Our thanks also go out to the hard-working administrators, teachers, students, parents, and RTI coaches from Colorado Springs School District 11. Without their enthusiasm and dedication, RTI would not be effective.

A special thanks goes to Cynthia Martinez (principal of Carver Elementary School), George Ewing (principal of Hunt Elementary School), and Brenda LeBrasse (principal of Holmes Middle School) for the use of their schools' data. An extra thanks goes to the pilot and exemplar schools for their willingness to risk and change.

To learn more about RTI in Colorado Springs District 11, visit www.d11.org/rti.

Table of Contents

About the Authors

Robert J. Howell, Ed.D.

Bob Howell has over 40 years of experience in private and public schools and in corporate healthcare. His work includes leadership consultation with private and public entities in developing programs for children and adults with educational or mental health needs. He has been a practicing principal in the elementary and secondary school settings, and has led large districtwide initiatives in curriculum and instruction. His background includes teaching at the university level as an adjunct professor at California State University, Los Angeles, and serving as head of the education department at the University of Phoenix, Colorado Springs. He has conducted workshops, training, and in-services in the United States and Mexico. His major focus has been students at risk, including research findings, application of research to programs, program development, research, and evaluation.

In 2005, Dr. Howell was selected to take charge of a district-wide initiative to implement Response to Intervention (RTI) in a public school setting, specifically to increase student achievement for subgroups impacting adequate yearly progress under the No Child Left Behind Act. As part of this initiative, Dr. Howell secured funding for RTI evaluation and research using nationally known researchers. He also spearheaded local funding and implementation at more than 60 school sites.

Dr. Howell holds degrees from Brigham Young University (Ed.D. in public school administration), California State University, Northridge (M.A., National Leadership Training Program in administration), California State University, San Francisco (M.A. in special education), and Florida State University (B.S. in special education).

Sandra L. Patton, M.A.

Sandy Patton is a highly experienced educator specializing in instructional interventions, school library media, instructional technology, and 21st-century information and learning skills. Her broad-based K–12 educational experience spans over 40 years. Her key areas of strength are RTI, professional development, information literacy, 21st-century learning, educational reform, standards-based learning, strategic and organizational planning, and project management. Most recently, she served as project director of a districtwide initiative to implement RTI in a 60-site public school setting, specifically to increase student achievement for subgroups impacting adequate yearly progress under the No Child Left Behind Act.

Sandy has degrees from the University of Alabama (library science), University of Colorado (educational media and technology), and University of Denver (administrator licensure). She is a frequent presenter at state, regional, and national conferences. She serves on the board of trustees for the Educational Communications and Technology Foundation, and has served in leadership positions (frequently as an officer) with local, state, regional, and national organizations.

Sandy was selected as Educator of the Year for Colorado Springs School District 11, was awarded the SIRS Media Specialist of the Year from the Association for Educational Communications and Technology, and was awarded the Outstanding Service Award from the Colorado Educational Media Association. Sandy has also been honored as the Outstanding School Administrator for Colorado from the Colorado Association of Libraries.

Margaret T. Deiotte, BSB/PA

Margaret Deiotte's experience in business and education brought her to her work with nonprofit organizations. She has founded her life on increasing the capacity of nonprofits to be successful. She has been a consultant and grant writer to schools, school districts, and community nonprofits for more than 25 years. In 1997, she founded Outside the Box, a consulting firm specializing in grant proposal design, development and writing, strategic planning, program and project design, program evaluation, and now, RTI implementation. She regularly works with nonprofits in education, healthcare, social services, youth services, and the environment. Prior to founding Outside the Box, Margaret served as vice president of Logical Systems, a computer software firm.

Most recently, Margaret served as the program evaluator for the RTI implementation at a 60-site school district. She led the systemwide evaluation process, including interfacing with the external researcher. This was the first systemic research and evaluation of RTI in a large district setting. Margaret has a B.S. in public administration.

Introduction to Response to Intervention

Response to Intervention (RTI) is a system for educational redesign based on a hierarchy of interventions that are implemented to meet the needs of students who demonstrate underachievement in core academic areas of literacy and math. This system is usually represented graphically by a pyramid showing three levels or tiers of intervention.

Tier 3	INTENSIVE	1–5%
Tier 2	TARGETED	10–15%
Tier 1	UNIVERSAL	80–90%

ACADEMICS   BEHAVIOR

Student behavior, attendance, and school completion are also addressed in the pyramid in a plan for improvement.

The underlying concept of the pyramid design is that all students can learn, effectively master educational requirements, and graduate from high school as proficient learners. RTI differs from the more traditional school approach to student learning, which either ignores underachievement or virtually disposes of students with behavior and attendance problems (through neglect or highly aversive rules resulting in school dropouts). The RTI philosophy recognizes that all students will not master all academic requirements at the same level or in the same timeframe, or respond in the same way to behavioral interventions.

RTI serves student needs using a triage concept developed out of the medical model which matches needs to resources. First seen during the Napoleonic Wars, the triage system sorted soldiers in the field to different medical interventions based on the severity of their needs for treatment. Since then, triage has changed its focus from sorting the "savable" from those who could not be saved, to categorizing the type of and immediacy for treatment: It is "a brief clinical assessment that determines the time and sequence in which patients should be seen, the speed of transport and choice of hospital destination. These decisions generally are based on a short evaluation of the patient and an assessment of vital signs" (Derlet, 2004, p. 1).

In education, the triage model incorporates screening, assessing, diagnosing, and prescribing interventions, and finally treats the student's learning gaps. RTI moves a group of students with high risk of failure to a position of success. RTI's tiered structure identifies those students most in need of intervention early in their education, in order to avoid academic failure. It then provides them with short-term, increasingly intensive instruction until they are performing at least at levels of proficiency in behavior and in core academics of reading, writing, and math.

In its medical context, triage sorts the treatable wounded from those not likely to survive. Of course, in the United States, public education laws mandate that no child is abandoned academically. In the context of this book, *triage* means prioritizing the most critical learning gaps of each child to ensure that *everyone* survives with proficient basic skills in math and literacy.

RTI provides a rigorous and relevant curriculum, with rigorous instruction delivered in a mode geared to a student's needs. The RTI system monitors student performance and provides quality interventions as soon as performance drops below proficiency. Teachers continue performance monitoring, changing or adjusting interventions as needed. If, based on student data, improvement goals are not achieved, the student is moved to the next tier for more intensive help. High-quality instruction, combined with early and frequent interventions linked with regular progress monitoring, is the critical component that will finally eliminate the wait to fail system. It will also actualize the belief that all children can learn if given the right opportunity and time.

The origin of RTI might cause some educators to conjure up the sad endings of old war movies, in which nearly dead soldiers, too far gone to save, are left on the battlefield to die. Fortunately, we have come a long way in both healthcare and education. Educational triage—that is, RTI—"leaves no child behind." In fact, the RTI system has generated preventative approaches to literacy and math through early intervention using evidence-based practices.

RTI is not a short-term fix for low achievement. It is not a special education initiative. It is a multiyear journey of discovery that can shape the strengths of your school system into an explosion of student success. Expect to learn more for your students. Expect to change your school system forever.

Overview of This Book

Key Points to Remember

- Old systems were established on old beliefs that no longer work.

- Legislative labels are barriers to student achievement.

- A crisis in public education requires different skills and instructional redesign.

- The No Child Left Behind Act (NCLB, 2001) and the Individuals with Disabilities Education Act (IDEA, 2004) create a contiguous system for achievement.

- Discrepancy formulas and bell-shaped curves inhibit early interventions for students in need.

This book provides concrete guidelines for establishing RTI at the district, school, and classroom levels. The keys to developing a high-quality RTI system in an educational setting rest on using continuous quality improvement (CQI) management tools within professional learning communities (PLCs) to address the needs of *all* learners. This book provides a practical model for teachers, principals, district administrators, and parent advocacy groups, with clear examples of how to:

- Develop stakeholder support for educational redesign.

- Establish leadership at the district and school levels.

- Establish a school-based RTI Problem-Solving Team.

- Apply research-based practices.

- Garner parent involvement.
- Use data to monitor progress.
- Implement models of intervention.
- Implement the RTI model systemically and systematically. (We use *systemic* to mean the embedded policies, procedures, practices, and beliefs found vertically and horizontally within the organization. *Systematic* refers to those procedures and practices that are scheduled and followed consistently by district staff to ensure program fidelity and sustainability.)

The concepts and skills in this book are derived from the systemic and systematic work of implementing RTI in a school district with 60 sites. This could not have been accomplished without the past and current work of experts including, but not limited to, W. Edwards Deming and his work on continuous quality management; Richard DuFour, Robert Eaker, and Rebecca DuFour and their work on professional learning communities; Stanley Deno and Mark Shinn and their work with curriculum-based measurement; and researchers in the field of educational interventions, including Dan Reschly, Jack Fletcher, Dave Tilly, Sharon Vaughn, and Barbara Foorman. RTI builds on a strong foundation of educational management and practice.

We confronted an educational environment where the district's board of education was divided into two camps (pro-public education and pro-private school vouchers), with a superintendent in the process of leaving the district. The district exhibited low and flat student achievement over several years, with islands of student success. Federally mandated supplemental programs, such as special education, Title I, and English-Language Learner (ELL), functioned in silos with little collaboration on funding, resources, or instructional strategies. In spite of these odds, district leadership, the board of education, and staff members were committed to doing something different to abruptly improve student performance.

We learned the practical precepts of RTI firsthand as we struggled with establishing a way to impact flat and declining achievement in a large urban school district. The district faced external compliance regulations for NCLB with 25% of the schools on adequate yearly progress watch; subgroups of disabled, low-income, and minority students continued to fail, and community confidence in the schools lagged. We discovered that no single source could be pinpointed to attack these problems. As we began to develop the RTI approach and plan, it became clear that we were developing a system of educational redesign requiring top-to-bottom change, and that other approaches to student achievement would continue to fail if not redesigned appropriately.

Educational redesign is necessary for schools to be successful. Educational redesign is also hard work! It requires answering four important questions: What do students need to learn? What do we need to do in order that they learn? How will we know when they have learned? How will we respond when they don't learn (DuFour, DuFour, & Eaker, 2005)? Policy must be established at the school and central administration levels, and by the board of education, that states, "In our district, our school, and our organization, *all* students *will* learn, and we will do everything possible to ensure that *all* students *do* learn." This policy must be embedded in the procedures and practices of an organization or school to ensure that curriculum, instruction, and assessment are aligned with standards. A data system of progress monitoring must be easily accessible to organizational leaders, the board of education, and to staff, parents, and students. Data must be monitored regularly and must drive instructional change.

If the current forms of educational practice—including the segregation of students into categories, such as disabled, gifted and talented, ELL, Title I, slow learners, dropouts, at risk, and so on—were effective, educators would not be struggling now with failing schools. Educational redesign uses existing resources but reallocates them at the school level so that *all* educators are responsible for the success of *all* students. This book provides examples of RTI redesign and reallocation that have worked to move student achievement forward, in some cases dramatically and even in such a short period of time as a school semester.

The school and the classroom, not the central office, are where educational redesign has the greatest impact. This book incorporates:

- Specific strategies to assist schools in realigning their system into a tiered model in which students receive the greatest impact with limited resources

- Examples of effective instruction, including systems and checklists that school leaders and teachers can use to evaluate how they are progressing in implementing RTI systemically

- Structures and support materials for RTI leadership teams, problem-solving teams, parent involvement, and student self-monitoring of progress

- Procedural examples to facilitate district- and school-level RTI implementation

In covering these areas, we explore both the failures and successes of large system implementation, as well as our ongoing collaboration with and research from other leaders in the RTI revolution. We want you, the reader, to have what was not available to us—a basic nuts-and-bolts guide to RTI success!

Chapter 1
Common Questions About RTI

All adults involved in the education of students *must* believe and *act* on the belief that *all* students *will* perform at high levels, although not always in the same timeframe or with the same strategies.

What Is Behind RTI?

The 1975 enactment and implementation of Public Law 94-142, the Education of All Handicapped Children Act, now codified as the Individuals with Disabilities Education Act (IDEA), required states and local educational agencies (school districts) across America to guarantee a free and appropriate public education to children identified as having learning disabilities. Millions of dollars have been spent on the education of children with disabilities, yet problems remain. High dropout rates, low college attendance, and underemployment are endemic characteristics of the population of students identified as having learning disabilities.

Underperformance by American youth is not limited to students with learning disabilities. Poor student outcomes are rampant in the population of those American youth who may not have qualified as disabled through the Americans with Disabilities Act (ADA), Section 504, or special education. Poor outcomes demand attention for a redesign of services not only for students with learning disabilities, but also for those students who do not obtain proficiency in basic skills prior to leaving high school. In most cases, those students without learning disabilities are predominately of low-income, minority, or English-language learner (ELL) populations.

The current approach of either ignoring these students or waiting for them to fail before providing the attention they deserve can no longer be tolerated by educators, parents, boards of education, federal and state elected officials, or the public. Furthermore, intervening on these achievement gaps in student groups early and robustly is not only more cost-efficient, but also more effective.

What About No Child Left Behind?

No Child Left Behind (NCLB), similar to many attempts at educational reform, came from studies supporting growing concerns about public education. The cost of public education in the United States continues to increase at staggering rates while performance of some student groups remains stagnant, or simply declines. Typical of much legislative change affecting public education, little preparation was made to ensure that the ideals of NCLB could easily be implemented in old systems unprepared to go through the hard work of educational redesign.

Due to an unwillingness of the public education bureaucracy to reform and change, and paired with the passage of the No Child Left Behind legislation, schools have moved into the *age of accountability*. Without a doubt, accountability is the most significant trend currently facing all aspects of public education. Whether accountability is for student performance, closing the achievement gap among student subgroups, use of public funds, accessibility of data to parents and the community, or pay for performance, the taxpayer is demanding results and data *now*.

Can These Kids Really Learn?

With the passage of NCLB, the American educational system has begun to have high expectations for all students. This requires a change in the core belief systems of many teachers and administrators. For years, the citizenry has heard about "those students" who were not performing at an acceptable level. Frequently, the excuses offered revolved around the students' home lives or past educational experiences. Excuses were plentiful, even leading to the question regarding student genetics: Can these kids really learn? Disaggregation of subgroup data required by NCLB has forced these students to the forefront of performance concern.

Research shows that *all* students, with minimal exceptions, can and will learn with the right strategy or intervention, but not always in the same timeframe or in the same way as other students (American Association of School Administrators, 2002; Carter, 2004; Education Trust, 2004; Togneri & Anderson, 2003). Schools and school staff must change the existing "bell curve" belief system, fostered by the idea that some children must fail, and instead actualize the belief that all students will perform at high levels, provided they are taught using a relevant and rigorous curriculum delivered in a differentiated instructional environment. Deborah Meier had this to say with regard to the need for a change in belief systems:

> I was glad when the word went out that schools needed to have high expectations for all children, that no kids should be labeled uneducable and written off. We would discover that every kid is smart—if we could tap into their smartness and make it work for them. If we weren't succeeding with all kids, then it was the schools that had to change—us, their teachers, our routines, our books, our ideas. And maybe we had to change dramatically. (Meier, 2002, p. 147)

How can educators, administrators, and parents make this belief system a reality? We believe, and research demonstrates, that with RTI, schools can move all kids to new and higher levels of performance.

Compelling Research

One compelling reason to employ a Response to Intervention system in schools is based on the exciting research findings reported by Fletcher, Foorman, and others (Fletcher, Fuchs, Lyon, & Barnes, 2006; Foorman, 2003). The research completed under the auspices of the department of neurosurgery at the University of Texas Health Science Center at Houston examined changes in the spatiotemporal brain activation profiles of individual dyslexic children associated with successful completion of an intensive intervention program. Eight children (ages 7 to 17 years old) received magnetic source imaging brain scans before and after 80 hours of intensive remedial instruction in reading. All of the children were previously diagnosed with dyslexia, a reading disorder characterized by severe difficulties in word recognition and phonological processing. Another group of eight children formed a control group, never having experienced reading problems as "normal" readers.

Before the intervention, all children with dyslexia showed abnormal brain activation profiles with little to no activation of the posterior portion of the superior temporal gyrus of the brain (involved in phonological processing). Their profiles also showed an increased activation of the right hemisphere area. After intervention, in reading that demonstrated strong reading improvement skills for all students, activity in the left superior temporal gyrus increased significantly in every participant. No systematic changes were detected in the activation profiles of the children without dyslexia over time. Conclusions suggest that the deficit in functional brain organization underlying severe reading disorders can be reversed after intense intervention lasting as little as 2 months. This is consistent with current proposals that reading difficulties in many children representing a variation of normal development can be altered by intensive reading intervention (Simos, Fletcher, Bergman, Breier, Foorman, Castillo, Davis, Fitzgerald, & Papanicolaou, 2002).

The significance of this research cannot be underestimated. Educators know the importance of strong, early development of reading skills for students. During the first 3 years of school, students are expected to learn to read well; thereafter, they are expected to read in order to learn well. The act of reading appears to exercise the most efficient part of the brain so critical to reading abilities. Observable brain differences occur in those students who learn to read, with or without strategic interventions, while those who do not learn to read are left behind to the point that the development of the "reading" brain is negatively impacted. The brain, without structured reading skills, appears to use the right hemisphere to decode the written word.

Why Wait for Kids to Fail?

The current process used to identify school-aged students with learning disabilities under IDEA grew out of regulatory requirements designed to differentiate between students who had low ability or I.Q. and consequently low achievement, versus those students perceived to have at least normal abilities, in whom low achievement was not typically expected. Federal procedures later adopted by states required evidence of a severe discrepancy between achievement and intellectual ability in at least one important domain of academic functioning, usually reading. In this process, states developed what became known as a *discrepancy formula* that included the use of I.Q. and academic achievement tests. Students demonstrating severe discrepancies between intelligence and reading performance (the most common deficit) usually qualified for special education services. Those not demonstrating significant discrepancies (for the most part) received no intervention or limited intervention, and performed poorly in school.

Discrepancy formulas essentially dictated a *wait to fail* process because it usually took time, often 1 to 3 years, for students to demonstrate severe discrepancies (see chapter 7, page 106). These discrepancies were not only a result of a disability, but also the result of a lack of strategic intervention. Students who were not discrepant *enough* in their performance most frequently received no interventions, interventions without scientific basis, poor treatment fidelity, and/or little progress monitoring. Consequently, an additional group of students was also failing, due to educational neglect. These students had often received poor instruction and were often also children of poverty, minority populations, and English-language learners.

It is now known that the predictive validity of I.Q. tests for children ages 5–9 is questionable. I.Q. usually accounts for only 10–25% of the variance in reading achievement, particularly as a predictor of reading achievement in the early elementary grades (National Center for Learning Disabilities, 2005). Furthermore, discrepancy formulas are laden with other problems. Students "age out" after age 9, when I.Q. tests become less reliable. Students from nonwhite, non–middle class back-grounds are overidentified, as are children with learning disabil-ities. Regardless, American education has not adequately met the needs of a large number of students with disabilities and typical peers who fail in school; these kids consequently leave school with huge achievement gaps that almost guarantee fail-ure in the typical accomplishments of life after graduating or dropping out. On the other hand, research demonstrates that virtually all students (about 95%) who enter kindergarten and elementary school at risk for reading failure can learn to read at average or above-average levels (Reschly, 2003; Foorman, 2003). However, success is possible only if students are identi-fied early and provided with research-based instruction.

Left to struggle without adequate intervention in the educa-tional system, nearly three quarters of students at risk will have difficulty reading throughout their lives (National Center for Learning Disabilities, 2005). Even more devastating, in the early years of education these students are unable to gain the knowledge from reading that provides essential subject matter familiarity and skills. Students at risk become mental drop-outs, demonstrate behavior problems, and develop severe self-esteem issues. After age 16 (the required school attendance age in most states), many of these students drop out of school, become involved with illegal drugs or chronically involved with the legal system, and certainly are underemployed.

What Are the Core Principles of RTI?

The following core principles were developed as part of the *Policy Considerations and Implementation* manual written by key RTI practitioners and researchers in conjunction with the National Association of State Directors of Special Education (Batsche, Elliott, Grimes, Kovaleski, Prasse, Reschly, Schrag, & Tilly III, 2005):

- **We can effectively teach all children.** This core principle goes back to the foundational belief that *all* children can learn. Furthermore, educators are derelict in their responsibility when they fail to see all children as *their* children.

- **Intervene early.** Wait to fail does not work. The earlier the problem identification and intervention, the better—this means beginning in kindergarten. When learning problems are not identified in kindergarten, not addressed until first grade, and not measured until second grade, students are already 2 years behind. These students who are 2 or more years behind in reading usually fail to ever catch up with peers. Highly effective diagnosis and intervention in grades K–3 are critical to building a student's foundation to learning for the remainder of his or her education and work experience.

- **Use a multitier model of service delivery.** One size rarely fits all; certainly that has not worked in public education. The model of service delivery must be based on student need. Differentiation of curriculum and instruction is not easy, but it is vital to support successful learning for all children.

- **Use a problem-solving method to make decisions within a multitier model.** Research has shown that the use of a Problem-Solving Team to diagnose and prescribe interventions is an effective tool to help students perform (Batsche, Elliott, Grimes, Kovaleski, Prasse, Reschly, Schrag, & Tilly III, 2005). The team must define the problem, determine why the problem exists, identify interventions to solve the problem, use frequent progress monitoring to determine if the intervention is working, and finally, modify or change the intervention when needed.

- **Use research-based, scientifically validated instruction and interventions to the extent available.** This is a requirement of both NCLB and IDEA, but even more important, it is good for kids. Research-based, scientifically validated curriculum, instructional strategies, practices, and interventions that are used with fidelity ensure that students are provided high-quality learning opportunities.

- **Monitor student progress to inform instruction.** What better way to determine if students are learning than to look at the students' artifacts? This is accomplished by using curriculum-based measurements that can be easily administered but are sensitive to small changes in student performance—and by looking at student work on a systematic basis.

- **Use data to make decisions.** Data must be easily accessible, understandable, relevant, current, and accurate. RTI fails when data do not conform to these requirements, thus rendering the data unusable by teachers, administrators, and parents.

- **Use assessment for three different purposes.** RTI uses three types of assessments: 1) *screening* to determine if a student is making the expected progress both academically and behaviorally, 2) *diagnostics* to determine what the student can and cannot do, and 3) *progress monitoring* to determine whether the intervention is producing the desired effects.

RTI is the practice of 1) providing high-quality instruction matched to student needs and 2) using learning rate over time and level of performance to 3) make important educational decisions (Batsche, Elliot, Grimes, Kovaleski, Prasse, Reschly, Schrag, & Tilly III, 2005).

Is RTI Just for Special Education Students?

Although RTI has its roots in special education, it is an integrated general education approach that *includes* special education, English-language learners (ELL), gifted and talented, and Title I programs. It is, first and foremost, an initiative to be used with all students and in the general education classroom. Effective implementation requires collaboration by all factions of the educational community so that no group or subgroup of students is left out. NCLB requires measurable and improved student outcomes—deliverables that RTI can provide.

The special education roots for RTI can be traced to two recommendations made by the President's Commission on Excellence in Special Education (2002) report, *A New Era: Revitalizing Special Education for Children and Their Families*:

- "Consider children with disabilities as general education children first . . . in instruction, the systems must work together to provide effective teaching" (p. 13).

- "Embrace a model of prevention, not a model of failure. The current model guiding special education focuses on waiting for a child to fail, not on early intervention to prevent failure. Reforms must move the system toward early identification and swift intervention, using scientifically based instruction and teaching methods" (p. 9).

The President's Commission goes on to say, "Implement models during the identification and assessment process that are based on response to intervention and progress monitoring. Use data from these processes to assess progress in children who receive special education services" (2002, p. 21).

Special educators first conceptualized RTI as a way of working with struggling learners. They then recognized the need to expand the approach to all students and all classrooms. When implemented with fidelity RTI plays a key role in identifying and working with struggling learners in any setting, and ultimately helps educators make better decisions about which children should be referred for additional targeted assistance.

What Are the Three Tiers of Intervention?

The RTI model provides three tiers of best practices within the educational setting. Consider student intervention as a triangle, shown in Figure 1-1, divided horizontally into three unequal sections. The tier at the bottom of the triangle, Tier 1, includes most students (80–90%). When presented with best instructional practices in a universal classroom setting, most students will perform proficiently as evidenced by assessment outcomes.

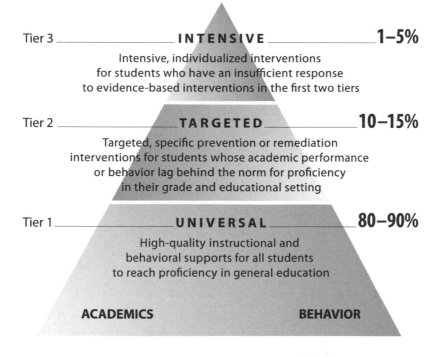

Tier 3 ——————— **INTENSIVE** ——————— **1–5%**
Intensive, individualized interventions
for students who have an insufficient response
to evidence-based interventions in the first two tiers

Tier 2 ——————— **TARGETED** ——————— **10–15%**
Targeted, specific prevention or remediation
interventions for students whose academic performance
or behavior lag behind the norm for proficiency
in their grade and educational setting

Tier 1 ——————— **UNIVERSAL** ——————— **80–90%**
High-quality instructional and
behavioral supports for all students
to reach proficiency in general education

ACADEMICS   **BEHAVIOR**

Figure 1-1. RTI Multitiered Intervention Model

Students who struggle in Tier 1—students who are not growing at a pace equal to peers, or at the rate to reach proficiency—are provided additional differentiated instruction, smaller groups, and other best-practice interventions within the regular classroom setting while continuing to move with other classmates toward proficiency at a rate commensurate with schoolwide success. Instruction and interventions can be provided by the classroom teacher or may be delivered by a team of interventionists already available at the school. These individuals are trained in specific skills in reading, writing, math, English-language learning, and behavior development. In some schools, these individuals are also general educators, special educators, professional tutors, and volunteers. These efforts are designated as Tier 2 or the targeted tier, the middle section of the RTI triangle, which serves approximately 10–15% of all students. Instruction in Tier 2 is delivered with greater frequency, intensity, and duration *in the areas of deficit* than those in Tier 1.

For students who continue to demonstrate lagging performance in Tier 2, the third tier at the top of the triangle provides the most intensive interventions. Tier 3 serves about 5% of all students. Instruction is highly specific, addressing the root causes of poor performance, and is provided with increased frequency and intensity. Generally speaking, this tier serves students in special education, ELL classes, and those with significant skill deficits. No student is denied services based on a label or lack of label. The goal is, *"All* children learn at our school and in our school district at a pace geared to closing the achievement gap before high school graduation."

All children can learn. This goal is based in fact! Research from the Education Trust, and findings of educational researchers, reading experts, and psychologists demonstrate that when provided a rigorous curriculum aligned to standards, scientifically based instruction and interventions, a high-quality learning environment, and curriculum modifications based on monitored progress, children learn at a rate at least comparable to advantaged peers (Education Trust, 2004; National

Center for Learning Disabilities, 2005; Scanlon, Vellutino, Small, Fanuele, & Sweeney, 2003). We discovered the practical application of these research findings in our own work when two groups of students (one from special education and one from general education) from low socioeconomic backgrounds demonstrated a rate of growth exceeding their peers who were not in RTI instructional services. In some cases, a year's growth was demonstrated in one semester. Other controlled studies demonstrated similar findings that students, when provided strategic reading interventions, grew at a rate that surpassed their past performance and at a rate above their peers. Were these students products of instructional errors over time, or were they truly students with learning disabilities? Clearly more research is needed and will help clarify those questions.

As the research demonstrates, the essential concepts of redesign came from the failure of special education to meet expected student achievement gains under previous approaches. Even with the enriched resources provided to special education groups, student achievement was not significantly impacted.

The needs of underachieving students are similar despite ethnicity or socioeconomic status or the presence or absence of categorical labels such as *Title I*, *ELL*, or *learning disabled*.

Why Is the Problem-Solving Team So Important?

The use of a structured Problem-Solving Team is a critical component of RTI. A structured, systematic problem-solving process—*root cause analysis*—facilitates the identification and diagnosis of student learning needs. The team must analyze data, diagnose the learning problem, prescribe interventions to solve the problem, recommend the type and frequency of progress monitoring, and decide when the team will assess the results. This process is discussed in depth in chapter 3.

How Do We Know RTI Is Working?

Schools certainly cannot have an effective problem-solving process without a strong assessment component. Assessment is directly linked to several strategic purposes—screening, diagnostics, and progress monitoring. For RTI purposes, screening (also called benchmarking) is an assessment given to all students, usually three times per year, with the definite purpose of identifying as early as possible students who are not performing up to expectations and assessing the effectiveness of a student's instructional program. Students identified through benchmarking are provided with diagnostic assessments to determine which skill strengths and deficits they may have. As targeted interventions are provided, progress monitoring is employed to evaluate the effectiveness of the interventions and to determine the intensity of interventions needed. In other words, schools need to identify students as early as possible, provide high-quality instruction, and introduce interventions as demanded by the data from progress monitoring. Curriculum-based measurements (CBMs) are easy to administer, and are sensitive to small changes in performance; therefore, they seem to be a logical tool to use in a Response to Intervention process.

Curriculum-based measurements are formative assessments that directly measure student performance within the existing curriculum. Most often, CBMs are used to measure the progress of student achievement in the basic skills of core academics—reading, writing, spelling, and math. However, with careful construction, CBMs can be created and normed for any curricular area.

A knowledge of the principles and concepts behind RTI is essential for successful implementation. However, knowledge alone is not enough. Strong leadership at both the building and district levels is critical. The next chapter discusses the leadership components of RTI.

Chapter 2

Leadership

In order for RTI to be effective in raising student achievement, strong leadership must be provided by the board of education, the superintendent and his or her staff, and school principals and staff.

Educational leaders commonly attempt to downplay the far-reaching requirements of leading change for RTI. RTI is educational reform; it is not as often described as just *good instruction*, nor just *reframing* what we already do, in different terms. It takes brave, risk-taking leaders to develop environments where RTI will be successful. Of course, the only reason to implement RTI is to aggressively improve student achievement, particularly for those groups who fall at the lower end of the achievement gap. Therefore, dramatic change in the results of student achievement will most often require dramatically different functioning on the part of people involved in educational systems—teachers, administrators, support staff, boards of education, superintendents, and central office staff. These kinds of changes take powerful leaders who know how to support and lead educational reform successfully.

Kenneth Leithwood reflects, "Leadership has significant effects on student learning, second only to the effects of the quality of curriculum and teachers' instruction" (Leithwood & Riehl, 2003, p. 2). There is overwhelming evidence that strong leadership is provided by 1) setting direction, 2) developing people, and 3) developing the organization. For educational redesign to be successful, the board of education, superintendent and his or her staff, and school principals and site-based leaders must have the passion and capacity to lead. As Leithwood and Riehl go on to say, "While the mastery of these basics provides no guarantee that a leader's work will be successful in a particular school district context, lack of mastery likely guarantees failure. A successful leader needs to do more but cannot do less" (2003, p. 5). Consequently, these three levels of leadership—the board of education, district superintendent and administration, and school site leadership—must be aligned to enhance success and minimize failure in the RTI paradigm.

The Board of Education

The board of education must set direction through policies and regulations that affirm the conditions set forth previously. Specifically:

- All students can learn, as demonstrated by closure of achievement gaps.

- Early and ongoing intervention leads to student success, as demonstrated by increasing student performance from unsatisfactory, to partially proficient, to proficient, to advanced.

- Data must inform instruction; business is done differently based on an environment focused on student learning needs versus teaching needs.

- An effective board of education policy communicates school district direction, as in the example:

  The Walnut Valley School District board of education affirms the belief that all students must be provided the opportunity to attain their highest level of achievement. In this regard, the board of education requires that each school develop an RTI system that provides the interventions necessary for students to be highly successful academically and behaviorally.

District Superintendent and Administration

The superintendent and his or her staff must be knowledgeable and able to demonstrate the core components of RTI before they can lead in development. Perhaps the best illustration is for them to be able to ask and answer the following questions:

1. If we truly believe that *all* students can learn, what does that look like in our organization?

2. If we believe that early and ongoing intervention leads to student success, what does that look like?

3. If we believe that data inform instruction and lead to student success, what does that look like?

District Round Table

Based on our experiences in designing, developing, implementing, and evaluating RTI in large urban school districts with diverse student bodies and staff, we recommend that the superintendent appoint a District Round Table Team to provide leadership in the design, development, implementation, and evaluation of the RTI system. This team will be responsible for answering the critical three questions discussed. The team should include, at minimum:

- **The superintendent or designee** who has the authority to make decisions, garner resources, hold individuals accountable, and lead and monitor collaborative decision-making.

- **The leader(s) of curriculum and instruction,** including content and specialty program staff such as special education, Title I, English-language learners, gifted and talented, and so on—these individuals must be leaders not only by title, but also by the respect earned from peers and teachers through many accomplishments in student achievement leadership and collaborative problem-solving.

- **The assessment leader** of the district who is responsible for high-stakes testing concerns and knows the requirements of strategic monitoring and progress monitoring and evaluation. These functions include, but are not limited to, disaggregating the results of high-stakes assessments, comparison of high-stakes testing with normed achievement tests, ensuring valid and reliable curriculum-based measurements for progress monitoring, establishing district baseline data for grade levels and schools, and making these data relevant to district staff in a time-sensitive manner.

- **Teacher representatives** with skills in core curriculum and specialty programs—these individuals are not only critical for credibility but also instrumental in the rollout of the RTI program. It is helpful that at least one teacher also represents the teacher's organization or union, if appropriate.

- **Educational support staff,** such as literacy and math coaches, library staff, and instructional aides to support and expand the resources required to provide the appropriate materials and assistance to student interventions—representation by a classified instructional aide organization or group can also be helpful because the role of aides becomes providing instructional support in RTI.

- **Parental representation** through parent teacher organizations and building and/or district-level accountability teams, which are critical to building broad-based parent support.

- **Principals representing pre-K–12 education**—these individuals may not be the usual leaders selected in district initiatives. Principals should be selected based on their demonstrated commitment to diverse populations, leadership at their sites, and ability to lead school staff and other principals.

Sincere, quality collaboration can almost ensure success; its absence is highly predictive of the demise of RTI. An attempt was made at early collaboration in our own district; however, district leadership did not take a hands-on approach to this change, the superintendent moved on, and the group work failed. It was not until the board of education demanded results that the leadership modeled change and the correct pieces of RTI quickly began to fall into shape. We encourage building the commitment to infrastructure prior to moving ahead with the RTI initiative.

This book is designed to be used by the District Round Table Team so that design and implementation can begin with structural support of leadership, and without the often frustrating experience of "building the plane while in the air." This team must accomplish the following work to ensure a strong RTI foundation:

1. **Work with the board of education to provide the necessary information and skills to set policy.** This includes, but is not limited to:

    a) Ensuring that the precepts of strong and appropriate board leadership are in place or at minimum, are developing, by setting policy and requiring accountability

    b) Studying research behind student achievement in high-risk and affluent settings, which demonstrates that leadership must be active and accountable to create and maintain change

    c) Studying research regarding the impact of scientifically based interventions on student achievement as well as research on leadership requirements, and understanding federal and state laws regarding identification of students

    d) Visiting successful RTI schools, reviewing federal and state publications, and becoming knowledgeable about the ongoing work in the field of RTI

    e) Completing book studies about RTI, which can assist in opening honest and rich dialogue about the need for change and for sustaining redesign

2. **Establish a multiyear District Round Table commitment for RTI study and implementation.** The Round Table has at minimum 3 years of work to analyze district gaps, create an action plan, and implement RTI across the school district. Team members should

be assigned staggered terms of commitment such that some members participate for 1, 2, or 3 years. This process allows for the collective knowledge of the team to move forward each year, as well as for rotation of staff and the placement of committed members into the field to assist with school-level implementation.

3. **Develop Round Table norms and expectations.** These norms involve not only the usual housekeeping requirements of teams, but also the assurances of attendance, participation, and follow-through on assignments. Members must commit to the necessary professional development to provide leadership to the initiative. The superintendent must allocate sufficient funds, resources, and planning time for the team. The team must ensure that regular updates are available to the team members and the superintendent.

4. **Develop a logic system.** This system will serve as a roadmap from the district's current status through RTI goals, needed resources, measurable objectives, strategies, and outcomes. Logic systems encapsulate the key elements of an initiative or program. A logic diagram provides a graphic representation, usually on one sheet of paper, linking the needs of the child, school, or system to the desired end result. The logic diagram includes the purpose of the project, its current status, goals, targets, and expected outcomes. It helps everyone to see the resources required, in both human and fiscal terms. It is a roadmap of where the organization has been, where it is going, and why. More importantly, it describes what it will take to get there, and how the organization will know it has arrived at its targeted outcomes. Unfortunately, this step is often left out of district strategic planning. (See appendix B, pages 162–163, for a sample.)

5. **Establish the "look fors."** Look fors are the outcomes that can be observed from RTI implementation and fidelity. Perhaps the most critical step to the RTI initiative for the district is to have a true picture of what RTI will look like when beliefs and practices are in place. This is a brainstorming and focusing process to identify and describe the critical elements of curriculum, instruction, leadership, and assessment under an RTI framework that develops a foundation for root cause analysis (see item 6). It is strongly recommended that district staff and community *also* be given the opportunity to provide data to this planning process through a structured design process (see "A Structured Design Process to Establish 'Look Fors' in RTI" on page 26). The Round Table should gather this information through team focus groups and then aggregate and distribute the findings to the board of education and all stakeholder groups. During RTI implementation, these "look fors" become the basis for RTI implementation components as well as tools for formative and summative evaluations.

6. **Conduct a root cause analysis at the district level.** *Root cause analysis* is an eight-step process to discover and prioritize the key factors impeding district achievement. The analysis process focuses district-level change on the two or three key areas most likely to make the most significant differences in student learning. In most districts, the Round Table will probably discover that the improvement of effective Tier 1 (classroom instruction and classroom behavior management) is the lynchpin for change. (For more details about root cause analysis, see chapters 3 and 9.)

7. **Establish the implementation of objectives, strategies, tasks, timelines, and resources based on a root cause analysis action plan.** Assignments can be delegated to Round Table members or to an ad hoc implementation team to work on the specific element requirements. Due to the large number of school sites, our district chose to create an implementation team that focused and organized resources at the district level to support school-level implementation, served as a conduit for professional development and communication, and gathered evaluation data. We garnered multiyear funding from several sources during our 3-year RTI implementation phase. School teams were trained in 32 hours of rich professional development, including:

   a) The purpose, research, and structural requirements of RTI

   b) The dramatic research behind early intervention, particularly in reading

   c) The use of data to inform instruction through curriculum-based measurement (teachers can use this method to assess student progress in core academic areas) and Positive Behavior Support (an approach to helping students improve difficult behavior)

   d) Leadership requirements to establish RTI and Problem-Solving Teams that work

These seven elements are critical to the development and efficacy of systemic RTI. *How* the elements are designed and implemented may look different from district to district. The Round Table should encourage creativity of school teams and consistently reinforce fidelity of treatment in the design of RTI at the district and school levels.

A Structured Design Process to Establish "Look Fors" in RTI

The RTI design process uses the three questions originally posed to the District Round Table. Round Table focus groups provide information as to what observable and measurable features anyone would be able to identify if they "walked in off the street" and saw the district in action. The observables are not necessarily what the district now has in place, but rather what needs to be developed to get the critical elements in place with efficacy.

In our district, one knows we believe all children can learn because:

- The majority of students (80–90%) are proficient or advanced on high-stakes testing, and the remaining students demonstrate adequate yearly progress (AYP).

- All instructional staff can demonstrate high skills in differentiated instruction.

- The curriculum is determined to be rigorous as compared to districts of similar demographics, regardless of student populations representing children of poverty, minority groups, English-language learners, or students with disabilities.

In our district, *all* students are provided the opportunity to achieve academic and behavioral success through early intervention and ongoing intervention as evidenced by the following:

- The district has designed and implemented a literacy plan in reading, writing, and spelling that encompasses pre-K–12 instruction and is aligned to formative and summative assessments leading to high-stakes testing requirements and standards.

- A master plan of interventions has been designed for basic skills in language arts and mathematics, demonstrating a pyramid of intervention available to all students in need of educational intervention.

- Each school has a developed plan for school and classroom management with a pyramid of intervention designed to improve learning, and classroom management resulting in student academic and behavioral improvement.

In our district, all instruction is data-driven as observed by the following:

- All students receive annual baseline assessments in language arts and math to ensure that no student is falling behind his or her expected achievement towards graduation.

- All schools provide quarterly benchmark assessments to determine that students are demonstrating targeted achievement in core academics and advanced classes.

- The schools and district use baseline and quarterly benchmarks to review district, school, and classroom performance followed by appropriate adjustments to align the curriculum.

- Students demonstrating underachievement as compared to peers (norms) are provided

continued on next page →

interventions in a three-tiered model of intervention. Students in these tiers of intervention are provided short-term assessments to ensure that they are approaching or exceeding rates of improvement and achievement targets. These data are addressed in Problem-Solving Teams at each school, and adjustments to the student's individual program are made in response to data.

Periodic Review

The District Round Table should periodically review its own leadership skills in implementing RTI. It is helpful to examine the following facets: setting direction, developing people, and developing the organization.

Setting Direction

The District Round Table should ask, *How have we demonstrated that we are setting direction for the district?* This should be done by:

- Identifying and articulating a vision that supports beliefs that *all* children will learn, and believing that a developing learning environment is the tool to realize that vision

- Creating shared meanings through constant, open dialogue about the work being accomplished, successes, and failures

- Creating high performance expectations through data analysis, feedback, and accountability at all levels of the organization (school board, superintendent and staff, and school site staff)

- Fostering the acceptance of group goals by acknowledging successes, loudly and sincerely, of leaders and peers

- Monitoring organizational performance through data discussions and accountability processes

- Communicating through written, electronic, and verbal avenues; keeping the goals, shared visions, successes, and progress at the forefront of the organization's messages

Developing People

The Round Table should also ask, *How are we increasing the long-term leadership capacity of key individuals?* This should be done by:

- Offering intellectual stimulation through rich and challenging professional development that reinforces the importance of the work to be accomplished, and demonstrating capacity based on training with walk-throughs and peer evaluations

- Providing individual support through high-quality coaching and mentoring (principals must be the curricular and instructional leaders of RTI interventions and core instructional improvement)

- Providing appropriate models through leadership and exemplar classrooms and schools, in a safe and supportive process fostering group improvement

Developing the Organization

Finally, the Round Table should ask, *How are we increasing the capacity of the district to sustain excellence in academic achievement?* This should be done by:

- Strengthening school culture by 1) identifying the "look fors" at each school site that demonstrate the group is "walking the talk" and 2) sharing data on student and staff performance to demonstrate the accomplishments being made

- Modifying organizational structure by matching change to student-centered needs and moving from a teaching environment to a learning environment

- Building collaborative processes by ensuring that the group process leaders are continually "taking the temperature" of the group, and modifying processes toward group achievement (leaders must also ensure that individuals adhere to the vision)

- Ensuring that learning environments do not look like teaching environments—that they are student-centered, not staff-centered, and that core instructional needs and interventions supersede other environmental needs that are less important, such as bell schedules (even elective courses or specials become secondary to improving student performance through core instruction and interventions)

These components are by no means an exhaustive list of leadership requirements for school districts; rather, they are the core and minimal components that must be addressed by leadership for RTI to move from an initiative to an embedded, sustainable practice.

Organizational Resistance

Anecdotal reports from district RTI leaders in several different states reveal some consistent organizational resistance to RTI. Interestingly, this resistance does not usually flow from principals, teachers, instructional aides, parents, or students, but from central office staff. This should be an anticipated pushback because RTI is a revolution in traditional practices for curriculum and instruction and specialty programs. RTI is a different way of doing business, but it need not be threatening to anyone with the shared vision of improved student performance, ready to do whatever it takes to get there.

For example, curriculum and instruction leaders often pride themselves on internally developed curriculum guides. However, if 80–90% of students are not consistently performing at proficiency on high-stakes tests, and if the remaining 10–20% of students are not demonstrating adequate yearly progress, it is logical to assume that an appropriately aligned curriculum is not in place. The written curriculum and instructional practices and materials must align with standards and assessment practices if high-stakes testing outcomes are to be achieved.

Concurrently, school districts have seldom been able to blur the lines between specialty programs such as special education, Title I, English-language learning, and gifted and talented because of federal funding guidelines inhibiting group collaboration for all children. The most common deficit for underachieving students is language arts—reading, writing, and spelling. These are the common weak links among students in specialty programs as well. The use of early and ongoing interventions in five core categories of reading—phonemic awareness, phonics, vocabulary, fluency, and comprehension—benefits all of these students (Report of the National Reading Panel, 2000). Students' required sequential learning steps are more alike than different. We strongly support the study of strategic reading interventions for all teachers in preservice, and for existing teachers in inservice. Strategic reading strategies are not different based on the disability of a student, his race, his economic standing, or his low level of achievement. Specific instructional steps are required for students to strategically learn to read well. The art of teaching comes in to play when the teacher knows the student's needs so well that the correct intervention is provided. The teacher's knowledge of the student can be improved through the assessment stages of Problem-Solving Teams.

RTI builds on the key changes in IDEA 2004—an emphasis on prevention, which allows districts to eliminate the "discrepancy formula" in favor of tiered intervention strategies—and encourages resource blending because it maximizes positive outcomes for all students. Leaders of curriculum and instruction and specialty programs must work together collaboratively to ensure that the vision of *all* students learning can be achieved (IDEA Reauthorization, 2004). A districtwide collaboration plan for the deployment of staff for intervention and the delivery of services should demonstrate collaboration.

School Site Leadership

In addition to the District Round Table, individual schools must have their own School Leadership Team. This team may be new, or may consist of representatives from existing teams. To comply with state improvement plans, many districts have developed site-based leadership teams going by many names, such as the school improvement team, leadership teams, goal teams, or professional learning community teams.

School Leadership Team

Regardless of how it is established, schools should consider the following basic requirements for the School Leadership Team:

- **Multidisciplinary representation.** The School Leadership Team must include a cross-categorical representation of staff, parents, and, in high schools, perhaps students. The selection should include core academic teachers, parents, specialty teachers, ancillary instructors, and instructional support staff.

- **Multiyear commitment.** Just as in the District Round Table, it is recommended that this team have a distribution of terms from 1 to 3 years to ensure a broad base of participation and buy-in from staff, and rotation of expertise and experience. One elementary school used stipend money for after-school activities for staff leading the RTI process and the Problem-Solving Team. This was a shift in values, a *look for*.

- **Look fors.** As in the district design process, School Leadership Teams must identify what an RTI framework involves and how staff, students, and parents will recognize its systemic implementation. These points should be based on the district priorities, but should also incorporate key elements that reflect the individual school's starting point. For instance, one school might create additional look fors in the area of special education; another school might need to focus on disparately performing ethnicities. Look fors must include staff, student, and parent observable measures.

- **Environmental scanning.** We've found that the design process evokes significant discussion beyond achievement. Two typical issues are scheduling and Tier 1 classroom instruction. While these topics will be covered in more depth as part of chapter 4, they are worth some initial thoughts related to leadership. The RTI School Leadership Team must complete an environmental scan, perhaps using Looking at Student Work (LASW) methods, to answer the following questions: What are the key elements necessary for RTI success? What is already in place, and what needs to be changed? (LASW is an instructional gap analysis strategy that allows teachers to assess how well they are performing, based on what students are learning as evidenced by student work.) Be prepared to:

  - *Be creative.* One staff designated the music teacher and a special education teacher to set up the reading intervention plan for the school. Both had been trained in strategic reading systems.

- *Move periods and class times to match intervention needs.* Make sure intervention programs are used with fidelity and are not restricted by bell schedules.

- *Use* all *building staff to support teaming and interventions.* RTI can be accomplished with existing staff in most districts if silos of separation are removed.

- *Tackle issues of credits, curriculum alignment, and open communication.* Although state standards are often used as the scapegoat to restrict flexibility at the school level, in most cases, state standards and regulations are broad enough to allow for the flexibility required to implement interventions that students need and also allow for Carnegie credits and curriculum standards.

Once school staff experience the effectiveness of an RTI-based system, they become amazingly inventive. One small elementary school carves out early morning meetings; a middle school uses elective periods for mandated Tier 2 and Tier 3 interventions. Lacking a literacy curriculum (versus a language arts curriculum), a local high school placed students in back-to-back language arts/literacy reinforcement periods to ensure fidelity of interventions.

Issues of Effective Classroom Teaching

The School Leadership Team will cope with issues of effective classroom teaching. If it does nothing else, RTI exposes what's working and what's not in Tier 1. Be proactive. Empower the Problem-Solving Team (PST) to support classroom teaching. Create a process that ensures teachers have used and documented research-based interventions *before* they come to the PST. Ensure that the principal conducts effective, regular classroom walkthroughs as part of teacher evaluation. Document contacts and problem-solving with parents. With effective leadership, schools reduce the chance that all underperforming students are immediately classified as needing Tier 2 or Tier 3 interventions and sent somewhere else for remediation.

Periodic Review

The School Leadership Team should also conduct a periodic review (Step 8, the final step, of root cause analysis). Dimensions include the following: setting direction, developing people, and developing the organization.

Setting Direction

The School Leadership Team should ask, *How have we demonstrated that we are setting direction for the school?* This should be done by:

- Identifying and articulating a vision
- Creating shared meanings
- Creating high performance expectations
- Fostering the acceptance of group goals
- Monitoring organizational performance
- Communicating

Developing People

The team should also ask, *How are we increasing the long-term leadership capacity of our staff?* This should be done by:

- Offering intellectual stimulation
- Providing individual support
- Providing appropriate models through district and site-based collegial teams, such as professional learning communities, that aggressively manage the changes needed in school reform

Developing the Organization

Finally, the team should ask, *How are we increasing the capacity of our school to sustain excellence in academic achievement?* This should be done by:

- Strengthening school culture

- Modifying organizational structure

- Building collaborative processes

- Managing the environment

Each district and every school should have a list of exemplar behaviors that assist in the measurement of success; lack of measures will lead to failure. We have included one such example in appendix C (page 167) that lists observable group behaviors in one column, with degrees of accomplishment in four other columns ranging from "not evident" to "in place." This checklist is then used to identify exemplar sites and classrooms to support coaching of staff toward the sustainability of RTI as it continues as an embedded practice, as well as to make progress quantifiable and allow for root cause analysis to determine barriers to successful implementation.

> School environment is a critical component of academic achievement, particularly at the secondary level.

Behavioral Interventions

A Response to Intervention structure also incorporates behavioral interventions. We recommend tackling one side of the RTI triangle first—academics *or* behavior. While this book focuses on academics, the same general rules apply to either system. In our district, most schools staggered the implementation process, with years one and two focused on academics and years two and three adding behavior.

Positive Behavioral Interventions and Supports (PBIS, www.pbis.org) aligns well with RTI. PBIS is a system of operationally defined and valued outcomes, behavioral and biomedical science, research-validated practices, and systems change (National Technical Assistance Center on Schoolwide PBIS, 2008). Many district schools find that adding a tiered, data-driven behavioral system provides critical support for academic achievement. This has been particularly evident at the high school level, where academic performance (turning in homework, showing up for class) and appropriate behavior (social skills) overshadow or mask academic skill deficits. The School Leadership Team's environmental assessment should incorporate the behavioral aspect and should be a key delimiter in designing schoolwide change.

Final Thoughts

Clearly, implementing Response to Intervention for academic and behavioral improvement requires leadership from the board of education through and including the individual school staff. Although basic core quality principles must be in place to lead this initiative, all leaders will learn the required components of the RTI model through leadership activities. RTI is a reform that builds not only leadership skills in a broad base of district personnel, but also increases knowledge of basic instructional intervention skills required by teaching and instructional coaching personnel. While the board of education and parents also benefit from this knowledge, it is not at the same depth required by instructional staff and leaders. Knowledge for change is created through a rigorous, mandatory professional development program for all members of the educational community.

We strongly advise that districts and schools *do not wait* to gain the skills in RTI to build the models, but rather use the process to improve leadership skills and knowledge of RTI simultaneously. Quality leadership is built over time in ever-changing environments and conditions. RTI is a developmental process requiring the application of basic leadership skills along with continuous development of expertise in RTI fundamentals: professional learning communities, root cause analysis, and continuous quality improvement.

Problem-Solving Teams are employed to gather data, and then use that data to determine the root causes of learning difficulty; team members then create continuous processes to bridge those learning gaps. This will be the primary focus of the next chapter.

Chapter 3

Problem-Solving Teams

Problem-Solving Teams (PSTs) are not child study teams as in special education. PSTs use data to discern current issues that exacerbate failure, discover the root cause or primary problem(s), and create a continuous improvement process to close the gap between a child's performance and grade level, national norm, or expected achievement.

Many terms have been used to refer to an RTI team, including *instructional support team*, *intervention assistance team*, *building-level team*, and *student support team*. In this book, the term *Problem-Solving Team* (PST) will be used to encompass all such teams that utilize the RTI process.

RTI Problem-Solving Teams usually go in one of two directions. Some struggle to create the forms and processes for implementing RTI. This concrete step feels safe and logical when establishing a new school system. The downside is that teams may spend an entire semester focused on processes rather than on helping students. Other PSTs jump right in and start problem-solving for students. This mode usually produces positive student results, which move other building staff to support RTI. However, without a honed problem-solving process, the PST will be unable to effectively make recommendations for every low-performing child. Thus, we propose that PSTs learn and practice root cause analysis as a way to create a problem-solving process while immediately serving students.

Problem-Solving Primer: Root Cause Analysis

There are many problem-solving methods available under a variety of monikers. We believe that *root cause analysis* focuses on an ongoing problem-solving cycle rather than a one-time effort. PST members may waste time, energy, and precious instructional effort if root cause analysis is not rigorously employed as part of the RTI framework.

As previously noted, much of what is required to implement Response to Intervention effectively comes from other fields. Healthcare and risk management professionals have used the root cause analysis process since the 1940s to prevent disease and injury. The concept is easily understood—we can't solve a problem if we have not clearly analyzed its cause. Too often educators overlook the obvious causes of student failure because low expectations limit professional thinking and problem-solving to blaming the child or parents for lack of achievement. Once a group of educators becomes a true professional learning community, however, they must ask why students are not learning. Answering "why" requires a logical process of hypothesis testing that leads to prioritizing the causes of learning failure. The root cause analysis process requires eight critical steps (see Figure 3-1).

1. Define the problem based on identification of a sentinel event. A *sentinel event* is urgent and important and is a serious indicator of failure—for example, an individual student is falling significantly behind his peers in math, a classroom has done poorly on a formative assessment in writing, or an entire grade level demonstrates flat low-proficiency scores on high-stakes tests in reading.

2. Gather additional data and evidence about the problem.

3. Identify issues that contribute to the problem.

4. Delineate the possible root causes.

5. Develop solution recommendations for the primary causes.

6. Implement solutions to eliminate or diminish the causes.

7. Retest solutions based on data collection.

8. Review data from Steps 1–7 to determine systemic prevention or intervention strategies.

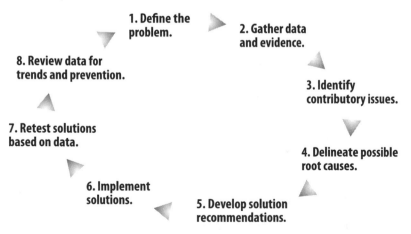

Figure 3-1. Problem-Solving Cycle: Discovering the Root Causes

An Individual Student Problem

Consider the following example of an individual student problem tackled with root cause analysis.

Step 1: Define the Problem

Fred's eighth-grade benchmark or pretest of math proficiency indicates that he is performing at the fifth-grade level and that he will not achieve proficiency in high-stakes testing by March.

Step 2: Gather Data and Evidence

The pretest demonstrates that Fred has low scores in test completion, number facts, beginning algebra, and word problems.

Step 3: Identify Contributory Issues

What might be causing his low student achievement, and where is this happening? Use the three Ws to assist in gleaning a rich body of evidence:

What?

- Instructional methods
- Instructional materials
- Measurement of student performance
- Curriculum linkage

Where?

- Place of instruction
- Time of instruction and quantity
- Quality of surroundings to support learning

Who?

- Readiness of the learner and motivation
- Skills of the instructor for delivery of instruction

- School culture and climate
- Parent support for learning readiness

In Fred's case, the PST finds the following:

- Additional analysis of student performance in reading comprehension demonstrates weaknesses in retelling and summarizing skills and vocabulary.

- Enrollment and attendance data demonstrate that Fred had poor attendance.

Step 4: Delineate Root Causes—Ask the "Why?"

Three-year-olds love to ask "Why?" repeatedly. They often do this until they get the answer they want. As adult educators, we ask why to get the best answer to the lack of student achievement. By repeatedly asking this, we can peel back the layers of symptoms and move toward root causes of a problem. Generally speaking, asking why five to six times will exhaust the possibilities and lead to root causes without blaming. Use the following steps:

- Write down the specific problem. Writing the issue helps formalize the problem and describe it completely. It also helps a team focus on the same problem.

- Ask why the problem happens, and write the answer down below the problem.

- If the answer you just provided does not identify the root cause of the problem that you wrote down in Step 1, ask why again, and write that answer down.

- Loop back to Step 3 until the team is in agreement that the problem's root cause has been identified. This may take five to six (or more) "whys." (iSixSigma®, 2006)

Let's apply these root cause analysis "why" questions to Fred.

Problem statement: Fred's eighth-grade benchmark or pretest of math proficiency indicates that he is performing at the fifth-grade level.

- *Why? #1 (Math):* Fred lacks computation skills in subtraction and division of integers and polynomials.

- *Why? #2 (Reading):* Fred lacks the comprehension skills necessary to read and interpret word problems.

- *Why? #2a:* Fred's vocabulary lacks the frames of reference and depth necessary to visualize the problem in context.

- *Why? #3 (Pre-Algebra):* Fred lacks understanding in abstract expressions, formulas, and equations.

- *Why? #3a:* Fred lacks the skills to understand patterns and number relationships.

Step 5: Develop Solution Recommendations

The PST identified two *primary* causes and one *subsidiary* cause for Fred's difficulty with math. This does not mean that there are no other contributing causes. There may be many, but the teacher and PST must concentrate on those that 1) will provide the greatest improvement in the shortest amount of time with the fewest resources, and 2) are within the purview of the school's control. In addition, the most critical issues must be tackled first. The PST recommends the following two solutions:

- **Solution 1**—Because Fred is at the end of middle school and already 3 years behind in basic skills, he requires a small-group (Tier 2) intervention in subtraction and division math skills in addition to his core math class. At the same time, he will receive additional small-group instruction targeting his reading comprehension and vocabulary skills in addition to his core literacy block. The frequency, intensity, and duration of these interventions will be documented in a Student Action Plan

(SAP) and adjusted depending on his progress, which will be monitored weekly with appropriate curriculum-based measurements (see chapter 5). Fred will also be counseled, along with his parents, on attendance and will receive positive reinforcement for improvement.

- **Solution 2**—Once Fred is making solid progress in basic math and reading, the pre-algebra gaps can be tackled. In eighth grade, this might be handled as a Tier 1 intervention since there will be others in the class with similar deficits. Specific intensity needs to be provided to improve Fred's skills in algebra readiness, basic concept mastery, and calculation speed.

Step 6: Implement Solutions

The eighth-grade PST and grade-level team develop a 2-hour block for Fred and other similarly identified students. In this block, students will receive intensive math interventions and literacy skills with emphasis on math word problem comprehension and vocabulary development. Weekly progress monitoring will be employed to demonstrate student progress in literacy and math using curriculum-based measurements based on content standards in end-of-year high-stakes assessments. Students are expected to demonstrate a progressive rate of growth sufficient for meeting end-of-year goals.

Step 7: Retest Solutions

If Fred does not demonstrate an adequate rate of improvement, as determined by the team in Step 5, he will be referred back to the PST for further root cause analysis and action plan refinement.

Step 8: Review and Establish Systemic Prevention

Root cause analysis findings from Fred and other students are evaluated on a regular basis. Trends and commonalities are used to improve class, grade-level, and school programs to ensure that all students reach proficiency in every subject, at or above grade level.

In contrast to a negative sentinel event, this root cause analysis process may be used for positive sentinel events. In a large urban district, for example, a third-grade classroom of students qualifying for free and reduced lunch was the only classroom in a district scoring 100% proficient on reading in high-stakes annual testing. What happened, and what was different? What would district leadership need to learn about this event that could have implications for other, lower achieving classes? Was the difference in instruction, curriculum, background, or behavior?

Figure 3-2 provides an example of how a PST might identify and analyze four potential environments—instruction, curriculum, background, and behavior—contributing to low literacy achievement. Instruction is identified as the root cause, thus the solution targets that issue first.

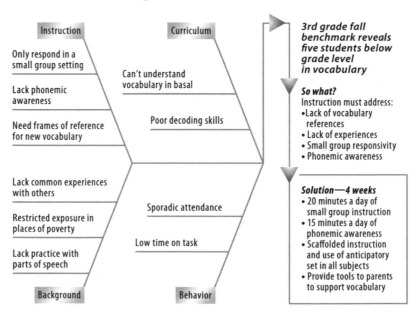

Figure 3-2. Root Cause Analysis

The example of Fred demonstrates that if the educators focus only on his lack of math skills or poor attendance, blame falls on previous educators or his parents. In an RTI model, the issue is problem resolution, not blame. PSTs use the collaborative power of professional learning communities to create the best realistic intervention opportunities for each student or group of students.

Creating a Problem-Solving Team

An RTI Problem-Solving Team is a diverse group of school-based personnel consisting of core and ad hoc members, including:

- Regular education teachers of various levels and disciplines
- School counselors
- School psychologists or social workers
- Instructional specialists, such as literacy coaches and lead teachers
- Special educators
- Referring teachers on an ad hoc basis
- Parent(s) of referred students on an ad hoc basis
- Principal/administrator as a team leader or chair

All PST team members should be knowledgeable in curriculum design, instructional strategies, and diagnosing and prescribing interventions. First and foremost, selected team members should passionately believe that all students can and will learn given time and appropriate help. Members should be well-organized, respected and approachable by staff, and experienced in using data to inform instructional decisions. Core membership of the PST should have 1-, 2-, and 3-year membership teams to ensure capacity-building and sustainability.

The PST meets regularly to address both academic and behavioral problems of children who are not performing at the proficiency level as measured on benchmark or high-stakes tests. The team is responsible for implementing a root cause analysis problem-solving approach to identify and intervene in response to students' needs within the arena of the general education classroom.

Developing a strong, stable Problem-Solving Team does not happen overnight. Teachers are accustomed to working in isolation and can be defensive about what they do and how their students perform. It may take considerable time and staff development to develop an effective, embedded problem-solving process. Teachers must be committed to the process in order for it to be a successful addition to the school culture. In our experience, it may take up to 3 years for the process to be formalized as a successful way of doing business.

After the core PST has been selected and the members have agreed to serve, the team needs professional development. Areas covered in professional development should include how to develop collaborative teams, consensus decision-making processes, root cause problem-solving, and rules of confidentiality that govern the operation of a team; professional development in intervention options should be available to the team as needed. Professional development must be provided to each new team member as the composition of the team changes.

Core PST members are assigned job roles. Except for the chair, these job assignments may be assigned for the school year or may rotate on a quarter or semester basis depending on consensus agreement of the team and wishes of the principal. Team assignments are:

- **Team leader (principal or administrator)** who leads the group to identification of the learning need(s) or discrepancy of a referred student; coordinates the diagnosis and prescriptive process for selection of the intervention to address learning needs; keeps discussions focused on the purpose of meetings; brings the group to consensus on the next steps; and delegates responsibilities to team members

- **Recordkeeper** who is responsible for scripting the discussion and decisions of the team and completing the hard copy or electronic intervention forms for the student (see appendix C, page 165)

- **Timekeeper** who is responsible for keeping the group on task and ensuring that the session is completed within the allotted time

- **Data manager** who reviews all pertinent information and data; organizes the most appropriate way to present the information and data at team meetings; and plots the goal line for a student

- **Case manager** who is responsible for interviewing teachers, parents, and the student when appropriate; collecting all pertinent information and data on the referred student; entering intervention performance data to monitor student progress (trend line); and comparing goal trend lines with class aim line and grade levels or national norms (see chapter 5 for sample graphs)

The following steps compose the basic process for PST members (see appendix C, pages 171–177, for sample forms):

- Obtain and complete the student referral form.

- Meet to review referrals, make team assignments, and set a PST meeting date for specific students.

- Notify parent(s) of concerns, and confirm the PST meeting date and time with parent(s).

- Complete the staff checklist or referral form.

- Gather relevant assessment data, graphs, student work samples, and cumulative data.

- Conduct a student interview.

- Conduct a parent interview. Ask parents to complete the Parent Survey.

- Meet as a PST—review data, conduct root cause analysis, and write the Student Action Plan (SAP).

- Schedule a follow-up review date for the targeted student no less than 2 weeks and no more than 10 weeks after the SAP is created.

- File the SAP in the student's cumulative folder (the team leader can complete this task).

- Review student success in follow-up meetings, and make necessary changes based on data.

Problems brought to the team should be defined as specifically as possible and in measurable terms. All pertinent data should be explored, and all appropriate and available interventions should be considered. The team leader must ensure that all parties understand not only the frequency, intensity, and duration of the proposed intervention, but also who is responsible for administering the intervention and who will enter all performance data. The PST should meet on a regularly scheduled basis in a designated location. (Note: As the team gains proficiency, the root cause analysis and action planning for each student should only take 20–30 minutes.)

Applying Root Cause Analysis

Response to Intervention applies root cause analysis problem-solving to address the learning needs of individual students. PSTs seek to resolve the learning discrepancies within the regular education classroom (at Tier 1) through the application of scientifically based interventions and systematic monitoring of student progress. This is accomplished through use of the eight root cause analysis steps.

Step 1: Define the Problem

PST members discuss the student referral information and define the problem in observable and measurable terms. The emphasis is to break down a broad general issue (problems with reading) into the specific skills related to the concern (problems with phonemic awareness, accuracy, fluency, or poor comprehension), thus providing a more specific and behavioral definition of the problem.

Step 2: Gather Data and Evidence

The PST identifies methods for measuring the specific problem identified in Step 1. This measurement, called a benchmark, identifies the preintervention level of performance. For example, if the identified problem is reading fluency, the team may decide to obtain a measure of words read correctly at a certain grade level in 1 minute. The reading probe is administered on three separate occasions, and the median number of words per minute is the student's baseline.

Step 3: Perform Data Analysis

The PST compares the referred student's baseline performance data to an acceptable level of student performance. This acceptable level is usually based on a class or grade-level norm that has been developed using measures such as curriculum-based measurement, but can also be measured against a state or national norm. Based on the discrepancy between the referred student's baseline performance and the expected or desired performance, the team can develop a Student Action Plan.

Steps 4 and 5: Develop and Implement the Intervention or Student Action Plan

The PST identifies evidence-based interventions to be implemented with the student, determines the frequency, intensity, and duration of the intervention, and identifies staff responsible both for carrying out the interventions and monitoring the student's progress. It is recommended that six to eight data points be collected on an intervention before determining its success or failure. Multiple data points are needed to determine the efficacy of the intervention, if the intervention is addressing the student's performance discrepancy and therefore, is successful. Progress monitoring might involve weekly or biweekly administration of the same type of CBM probes that were used to obtain the referred student's baseline. Resulting data can be plotted on the student's trend toward meeting the determined goal.

An intervention is a new strategy or modification of instruction or behavior management designed to help a student (or group of students) improve performance relative to a specific goal. In the context of this book, *interventions* are evidence- or scientifically-based strategies that have been proven effective in similar situations through well-designed research. Simply making a change is not really an intervention. For example, shortening assignments, contacting the parent, or moving the student's desk are not interventions, although a well-designed intervention might include such changes.

In addition to specific measurement of student performance, the Student Action Plan should address *fidelity* of treatment—the degree to which the intervention is implemented as researched and tested. This is critical when it comes time to evaluate the plan's effectiveness. If the intervention appears to be ineffective, it is critical to determine if the intervention really failed, or failed to be implemented as designed. An example would be using the Scholastic computer program Read 180® for only 30 minutes instead of the recommended 90 minutes. School building leadership and the PST should consider all factors—such as professional development and time needed for implementation—when selecting interventions to ensure fidelity of treatment. For example, if a tutoring intervention is recommended, consider critical factors such as availability of personnel, training for tutors, and space to work. *It is far better to have fewer interventions that are implemented correctly than a larger number done poorly.*

Steps 6 and 7: Evaluate the Student Action Plan

The PST analyzes the referred student's progress relative to the goal that was set in Step 3. Several different outcomes can occur when analyzing the data obtained during the intervention phase. If the team determines that the student is making adequate progress toward the goal or has achieved the goal as a result of the intervention, then the team may decide to continue the intervention with periodic progress monitoring without making any changes to the plan, or return the student to the regular classroom or course of study with no further intervention. However, continuation of progress monitoring is critical in order to identify any performance problems the student may encounter.

If the team decides that the student did not make adequate progress toward the goal with the current intervention after at least seven data points, then the team may decide to increase or change the frequency, intensity, and duration of the intervention or may recommend a different one.

After trying at least three interventions with fidelity and without improvement, the team may recommend moving the student to the next, more intensive RTI tier, trying an alternative curriculum, or referring the student to special education. The rationale for trying three interventions is rather arbitrary. However, in working with teachers and students, we found that one intervention does not provide adequate information for the team to recommend movement to another tier. Moving to a second intervention often means intensifying (more time, increased frequency) the first intervention. After three interventions, we believe that there is adequate data for the team to make valid educational decisions for the student. RTI should never be viewed as a way to get a student *out* of a classroom, but rather as a way to help him or her perform at an acceptable level *in* the classroom. Research indicates that implementation of RTI using the PST process can significantly improve student achievement and behavior while reducing special education referrals (Bergan & Kratochwill, 1990).

Step 8: Review for Trends

From a management standpoint, the PST, School Leadership Team, and District Round Table should investigate SAPs and outcome data for trends. For example, if 50% of students in fourth grade exhibit difficulties synthesizing text materials, the solution should be to change the classroom (Tier 1) instruction for all students. Other trends may reveal a weakness in curriculum materials or in schoolwide behavioral expectations.

Role of Parents

Parental input is critical to successful RTI Problem-Solving Teams. At least one parent of a student receiving intervention should be included in the team. Parent input often provides unique information, perspectives, and roadmaps to potential solutions for a student. PST meetings should be scheduled to support and encourage parental participation.

The PST is often instrumental in involving parents in home-based interventions. One elementary school we know encourages English vocabulary development in Spanish-speaking households by hosting potluck dinners and modeling vocabulary and reading skills during the meal. Another school built vocabulary and social skills into early morning assemblies lasting 10 minutes, kicking off the day for both students and parents.

Principal and Administrative Support and Involvement

Principal and administrative support and active involvement in the problem-solving process are critical. Active support and involvement show a thorough understanding of the entire RTI process and the key role that the PST plays in the successful implementation of this process. Principal understanding must be not only vocalized but also actualized in the form of resources—materials, staff development, and most importantly, time to conduct the process. In fact, an administrator, preferably the principal, must be a core member (team leader or chair) of the PST. This level of involvement carries the strong message to all staff members that RTI and the PST process are an integral part of providing for the learning needs of all students, and that participation is expected from all staff members.

Principals may no longer merely serve as managers of schools but also must assume the role of instructional leader. Gene Bottoms says it well in the article "What School Principals Need to Know about Curriculum and Instruction":

> Educational accountability has changed nearly everything. Superintendents and local school boards no longer can be satisfied with principals who simply place teachers in the classroom, provide textbooks and get students to attend schools. Increasingly, schools and school leaders are being judged on their progress in teaching all students to high standards that only the "best students" were expected to meet in the past. This means that future school leaders must have in-depth knowledge of curriculum, instruction and student achievement. (2003, p. 29)

We believe that knowledge of and commitment to the principles of RTI and PSTs and to the belief that all students can and will learn, given time and the right environment, must be part of a district's mandate to all principals and school building leadership. Principal support and understanding are as important to the success of RTI as good instruction and interventions.

Principals must provide guidance in the fidelity of the Problem-Solving Team process, and must also ensure that sufficient evidence-based interventions are available to the Problem-Solving Team. The next chapter provides in-depth information on the selection of interventions and their appropriate use.

Chapter 4

Interventions

An intervention is a new strategy or modification of instruction or behavior management designed to help a student or group of students improve performance relative to a specific goal.

The tiered Response to Intervention model is characterized by more intensive interventions and more frequent data collection as students move up the tiered continuum. Figure 4-1 (also shown in chapter 1) represents the common RTI pyramid, but school districts can benefit from developing their own "triangle" perspective and verbiage.

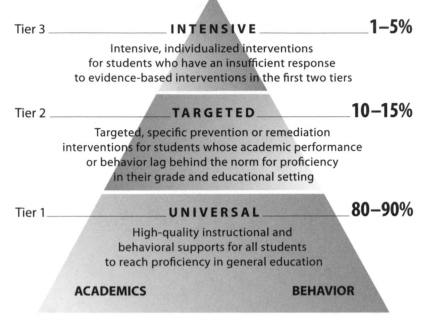

Tier 3 —————————— **INTENSIVE** —————————— **1–5%**
Intensive, individualized interventions
for students who have an insufficient response
to evidence-based interventions in the first two tiers

Tier 2 —————————— **TARGETED** —————————— **10–15%**
Targeted, specific prevention or remediation
interventions for students whose academic performance
or behavior lag behind the norm for proficiency
in their grade and educational setting

Tier 1 —————————— **UNIVERSAL** —————————— **80–90%**
High-quality instructional and
behavioral supports for all students
to reach proficiency in general education

ACADEMICS   **BEHAVIOR**

Figure 4-1. RTI Multitiered Intervention Model

Tier 1

Tier 1 or the *universal tier* is the general education classroom. It is characterized by high-quality instructional and behavioral supports that allow all students to reach proficiency as measured on high-stakes tests. Every classroom teacher uses a wide variety of interventions on a daily basis. The RTI model, however, organizes and assesses interventions that are available from the school's inventory and identifies which are based on research. The interventions are then organized into tiers with recommendations for frequency, intensity, and duration. Research-based interventions have many characteristics, including:

- An experimental design with a large sample size
- An experimental design that is documented in peer-reviewed literature

- A demonstrated correlation between the intervention and student progress

- Recommendations for how to deliver the intervention with fidelity

Interventions begin in the general classroom. Modifications include changing the intervention frequency, intensity, and duration until the student achieves success.

In the Response to Intervention model, all curriculum, instruction, and behavior interventions are selected on the basis of scientific effectiveness.

In Tier 1, all students are screened, and their academic progress towards benchmarks is monitored at least three times per year (pre-, mid-, and post-year) in order that performance problems are identified as soon as possible and appropriate solutions may be put into place. In large secondary schools, particularly high schools, screening three times yearly may be difficult. However, this should not be an excuse. Students may be identified based on quarterly tests built at the district level or standardized assessments such as the Northwest Evaluation Association's Measures of Academic Progress, semiannual tests such as TerraNova, or other high-stakes tests. Students below or significantly below proficient should be screened for baseline data. At the elementary level, academic screenings should focus on basic reading, written language, and math skills. At the middle and high school levels, screenings may encompass a broader range of skills and behaviors.

Tier 1 benchmark assessments should identify those students who need additional help to master the essential skills as defined by the district or state's curriculum. For identified students, additional classroom interventions are given as soon as the learning gap is identified. Differentiated instruction—altering the process, product, and curriculum to meet specific learning styles or learning needs of student groups—allows teachers to make sure that instruction corresponds to students' achievement levels and needs. Remember, *the quality of Tier 1 instruction and interventions will determine the success or failure of the RTI initiative.* If high-quality Tier 1 instruction and interventions do not address 80–90% of student learning needs, then Tiers 2 and 3 will be overwhelmed.

Interventions come in many shapes and sizes. They can be purchased programs, which are most commonly found in school districts. More importantly, they can be instructional strategies for when, where, and how teachers present curricular material, shape questions and teachable moments, and foster high-level thinking skills. Interventions may be simple or complex. Looking at Student Work (LASW) is cross-disciplinary and works with any instructional strategy. No matter which high-quality research-based instructional strategy is used in the Tier 1 classroom, LASW can help determine if students are learning what the teacher thought he or she was teaching. It also uses the power of the collaborative team in a professional learning community to improve the quality of general classroom instruction. For school leadership, it provides an environmental scan of classroom instructional practices.

Looking at Student Work: An Effective Tier 1 Strategy

LASW is much more than giving a student a grade according to a rubric. David Allen, a researcher at Harvard Project Zero and one of the authors of *Looking Together at Student Work: A Companion Guide to Assessing Student Learning* (Blythe, Allen, & Powell, 1999) said in a 2000 interview (*Education World*, 2000, p. 3), "Evaluation, which often takes the form of scoring or grading, is just one purpose of examining student work."

LASW is an instructional gap analysis strategy that allows teachers to assess how well they are performing based on what students are learning as evidenced by student work. Rooted in the belief that students can do no better than the assignments they are given, LASW helps teachers and school leaders inject rigor into standards-aligned assignments and maintain high expectations for all students. "The process of looking at student work in a collaborative manner helps teachers take a closer look at how they teach," Allen said (*Education World*, 2000, p. 5). If students are missing the mark and writing unsatisfactory papers or doing poorly on final exams, teachers need to find out why. In fact, most educators who look at student work in a collaborative process learn about the effectiveness of their instruction, better understand students' learning and development, develop more effective curriculum and assessment, and find ways to help students complete higher quality work (*Education World*, 2000).

Teachers still need to grade their students' work with traditional methods, Allen said, "but bringing samples of student work to the table with your colleagues, looking closely at them, and addressing important questions about teaching and learning has the potential to deepen teachers' understanding of the more traditional—as well as the innovative—work they do with students in the classroom" (*Education World*, 2000, p. 7). This process requires time, often no more than an hour a week. Schools should factor in time for teachers to work together in this way on an ongoing basis. In some cases, time is created during or after the school day; in other cases, it means shifting time already allotted for staff development, team planning, or other faculty work. We need to get beyond the mindset that teachers spend almost all of their time with their students or by themselves correcting papers and planning lessons. It is also important that they spend time brainstorming with colleagues regarding ways to improve their practices. "Time with colleagues spent in focused inquiry about teaching and learning is a necessity, not a luxury" (*Education World*, 2000, p. 9).

We subscribe to the *Standards in Practice*™ (SIP) protocols developed by the Education Trust (2007), which are:

- Discuss the purpose of the assignment.

- Analyze the demands of the task.

- Identify the standards that apply to the assignment.

- Generate a task-specific rubric (scoring) guide using the standards and the assignment.

- Score student work using the task-specific rubric (scoring) guide.

- Redesign assignment-plan instructional strategies.

In professional learning communities (PLCs), teachers collaborate to strengthen the rigor of their assignments and devise instructional strategies to match them. Together, they focus on four critical questions:

1. What do students need to learn and be able to do?

2. How do we know students are learning it?

3. What will we do if the students have not learned it?

4. What will we do if they have learned it? (DuFour, DuFour, & Eaker, 2005, pp. 3–4)

LASW creates shared norms, increases academic rigor, and provides an immediately applicable, effective way to help teachers change practices to get different results. The authors of "Looking at Student Work: For Teacher Learning, Teacher Community, and School Reform" put it this way: "Looking at student work has the potential to expand teachers' opportunity to learn, to cultivate a professional community that is both willing and able to inquire into practice, and to focus school-based teacher conversations directly on the improvement of teaching and learning" (Little, Gearhart, Curry, & Kafka, 2003, p. 229).

Because LASW provides real tools and very timely data with which to measure instructional rigor, the framework can be used as both an instructional design tool and an assessment tool. In fact, beyond its value as a Tier 1 intervention, LASW is a tool that the RTI School Leadership Team can use to determine the skills students should master based on the district's curriculum.

Other Tier 1 Academic Interventions

Other Tier 1 academic interventions include:

- Differentiated instruction—Altering the process, product, and curriculum to meet specific learning styles or learning needs of student groups

- Research-based strategies

    - High opportunities for response—Students have abundant opportunities to actively respond to and receive teacher feedback.

    - Choral response—Students in the class or group respond orally in unison to a teacher response.

    - Specific, continuous, positive reinforcement being provided.

    - Specific correction paradigm—A student makes an error, and the teacher stops the student and gives the specific correction before the student continues.

    - Brisk instructional pace—Teacher-led instruction is delivered at a sufficiently brisk pace to hold student attention.

- Peer and cross-age tutoring

- Additional instructional time in the deficit area

- Accommodations and modifications, such as use of assistive technology, different seating, modified curriculum, or alternative assessments

- Cooperative learning—"Small, heterogeneous teams, usually of four or five members, working together towards a group task in which each member is individually accountable for part of an outcome that cannot be completed unless the members work together" (California Department of Education, 2008, p. 4)

Behavior and academic performance, such as task attention or homework turn-in, may also negatively impact achievement. The following interventions can improve the learning atmosphere and expectations:

- Engaging family systems—Multiple ways for parents or family members to be involved in student education and learning

- High-quality classroom management
    - Consistent, clear expectations
    - Smooth transitions
    - Predictable classroom routines

- Specific, continuous, positive reinforcement

- Accommodations and modifications, such as use of assistive technology, different seating, modified curriculum, or alternative assessments

- Research-based strategies:
    - Proximity control—Student placed close to the teacher or another adult
    - Signaling to a student—Nonverbal cues between the teacher and the student to encourage student participation
    - Preferential seating—Seating the student in a location where he or she is most likely to stay focused

The key is to ensure that the interventions are based on research and implemented with consistent fidelity. We passionately believe that a strong Tier 1 instructional program is critical not only to the RTI process, but to the business of school. There are many instructional strategies and interventions that may be used effectively in the classroom. However, all teachers should have the knowledge and skills to differentiate instruction to meet the needs of all students. Districts should select a manageable number of evidence-based strategies and interventions, train staff for those strategies and interventions, and hold all staff accountable for implementing them in the classroom and learning environment with fidelity.

Tier 2

Tier 2 or the *targeted tier* provides more strategic interventions for those students who do not respond to Tier 1 instruction and interventions. When students fail to respond adequately in Tier 1, they are referred to the Problem-Solving Team for additional root cause analysis, including an examination of Tier 1 instruction. PST members work with the classroom teacher to determine if Tier 1 instruction was of high quality and if interventions were appropriate and delivered with fidelity, and to verify that the interventions did not obtain the results needed for the student.

Students are normally referred to Tier 2 after failing to respond to at least three Tier 1 evidence-based interventions. Typically, Tier 2 instruction and interventions are delivered in small groups, and data are collected more frequently. At this level, the classroom teacher and the PST monitor the effectiveness of the individualized interventions, adapting and changing them as indicated by data.

The Case of Sara

One way to determine the quality of Tier 1 practices is to evaluate a single student, Sara, compared to students in the same classroom. Over 80% of the students in Mrs. Elliot's classroom demonstrate good progress toward the aim of meeting high-stakes testing; as evidenced by the midyear benchmarks, Mrs. Elliot is meeting the instructional needs of most students. Mrs. Elliot provided four different interventions for Sara, varying the level of material and the frequency, intensity, and duration of instruction; however, Sara has not demonstrated an adequate rate of improvement that will enable her to meet or exceed grade-level expectations.

In the past, a referral to special education might have been made immediately for comprehensive assessments of social or emotional status, academic performance, and intellectual ability, often taking weeks to accomplish. The referral process would have included an evaluation of Sara's performance against her intellectual ability. The goal would have been to qualify or disqualify her (usually the latter) for additional services based on the discrepancy between the two. With RTI, the teacher and parent can refer the student to the Problem-Solving Team at her school. In this process, the team evaluates Sara's response to the intervention, taking into account her participation, the fidelity of the instruction, and the formative data collected from the use of curriculum-based measurements. Data for Sara and the class provide a baseline comparison. On a graph, the PST draws an aim line denoting expected class achievement levels (benchmark to end of year) versus Sara's projected achievement level (benchmark to end of year).

If this aim line demonstrates that Sara will not catch up to classmates or become proficient by the year's end, staff must supplement her instruction, causing an increase in the rate and level of skill acquisition. The PST now engages in the eight-step root cause analysis process outlined in chapter 3. Once the root cause or causes for Sara's low rate of improvement are established, the team identifies the specific interventions to correct the deficits. In Tier 2, these interventions begin immediately and are provided *in addition* to Tier 1 interventions. As needed, the Tier 2 interventions can increase in frequency, intensity, or duration, or be changed altogether until Sara is gaining at a rate greater than her classmates—one that will put her on track to catch up.

Let us say that Sara is performing 2 years below grade level in reading. The root cause analysis indicates low reading fluency and difficulty with pronunciation and comprehension of what she has read. The PST decides that Sara requires an intervention designed to increase her phonemic skills, comprehension, reading fluency, and vocabulary development. The interventions will be provided in a small-group setting of four students, daily (frequency) for 50 minutes (intensity) for 6 weeks (duration), for an additional 25 hours of instruction. Her progress will be evaluated weekly and plotted. (More information on using data is presented in chapter 5.)

If this plan of intervention results in Sara's progress approaching the same aim line as her peers, then intervention will continue until Sara is able to demonstrate strong skills maintenance. At that time, the intervention will fade or discontinue, and she will receive Tier 1 instruction only. If Sara does not demonstrate adequate improvement in Tier 2, then she will be referred for Tier 3 interventions.

Students in Tier 2 continue to receive Tier 1 instruction, keeping them on top of their grade-level coursework. They also receive strategic interventions that address their skill or behavioral deficits—in effect, double-dosing content and instruction. Only with significantly more time on task will students 2–5 years behind make the gains necessary to achieve grade-level proficiency.

Tier 2 interventions are most often modifications of those used in Tier 1. More importantly, they are used *in addition* to Tier 1 interventions.

Tier 1 +

    Increased intervention frequency (how often)

    Increased intervention intensity (group size or individual), or

    Increased intervention duration (length)

———————————————————————————

= Tier 2

Tier 3

Tier 3 or the *intensive tier* provides rigorous, individualized interventions for students who have an insufficient response to evidence-based interventions in the first two tiers. Tier 3 interventions may take place in regular *or* special education. At this level, the PST monitors the effectiveness of the individualized interventions and modifies them as needed. Again, students receive Tier 1 and Tier 2 instruction in addition to Tier 3 interventions. Tier 3 provides students with the greatest levels of intervention frequency, intensity, and duration in order for them to master literacy, math, and core academics.

Tier 1 + Tier 2 +

    Increased intervention frequency (how often)

    Increased intervention duration (length)

    Increased intervention intensity (group size or individual)

    Specialized interventions, or

    Alternative curriculum

———————————————————————————

= Tier 3

Does a student have to jump this hurdle of tiers before special education can be provided? Not necessarily. This is where the root cause analysis and the judgment of the PST members and parents are so critical. For example, one school district uses a rule of thumb that students obtaining high-quality instruction and interventions who still fall below the 10th percentile in normed curriculum-based measurements as compared to peers will benefit from the highest degree of intervention provided in special education. However, in an RTI system, special education need not be a life sentence. Regular formative evaluations of student performance toward an aim line of proficiency are most valid and reliable in determining referrals *out* of special education. The beauty of RTI for special education students, teachers, and parents is that the process does not brand students forever as "SPED" (special education) and maintains a belief that these students can learn effectively.

Special Education Concerns

Some special educators worry that RTI will preclude students with physical, sensory, or cognitive challenges from obtaining needed services. Others worry that "slow learners" will be overidentified as having a learning disability and flood special education services. In the RTI model, this would be an abuse of students. However, why would educators not apply the Response to Intervention system to most special education students in determining the application of *academic* and *behavioral* services within special education? If any student is able to achieve effectively in Tier 1 services, that evidence would be sufficient to determine services and placement. In the RTI model, inclusion can also be objectively evaluated and is used as a framework to determine where a student should be served, while addressing interventions of lower intensity in Tier 1 or 2 services and providing interventions of higher intensity in Tier 3 or special education. This RTI process also appears to make sense for inclusion practices, using frequency, intensity, and duration to determine the most appropriate setting for delivery of core academic and behavioral interventions versus using purely subjective information to make these decisions.

Professional Development Needs

Regardless of the tier of use, interventions should be matched to the learning needs of students, not based on what the teacher feels comfortable using. Teachers will need professional development to help them establish or hone skills in diagnosing and prescribing interventions to meet individual student needs. Staff development should also include training in the characteristics and features of strategies and interventions supported in the school district. Remember, *it is much better to have a short menu of strategies and interventions that can be supported well and implemented correctly than a long menu of options implemented without fidelity.*

Professional development and student behavior should not be overlooked.

Behavior in the Pyramid of Intervention

Response to Intervention, as a national movement, has taken the position that behavior is equally as important to the learning process as instruction is to academic learning. There is ample evidence that effective classroom and school management support high academic performance in students. All too often, low-performing schools demonstrate problems with student citizenship as evidenced by high percentages of non-attendance, office referrals, suspensions, expulsions, and dropouts. Unfortunately, these data also support the notion that those issues are more common in schools with high percentages of minority and low-income students (Borman & Rachuba, 2001). Schools functioning as professional learning communities have tackled this problem by reshaping the behavior and belief systems of the school staff.

Professional learning communities create collaborative teams where teachers and other staff members learn by sharing professional practices. They engage in conversation and deliberate about learning issues, including safe learning environments, thereby discovering original ways to resolve instructional and behavioral issues.

Data demonstrate that when schools adopt systematic and systemic Positive Behavior Support (PBS) systems and strong instructional strategies, untoward behaviors decline significantly (Sugai & Horner, 2005). PBS, a system of operationally defined and valued outcomes, behavioral and biomedical science, research-validated practices, and systems change has become an international movement and is recognized as a scientifically based tiered intervention system, perfectly aligned to RTI (National Technical Assistance Center on PBIS, 2008). For schools and districts interested in this program, PBS information is available at www.pbis.org.

Hunt Elementary School in Colorado Springs, Colorado, participated in our district's RTI research study. Hunt is home to 200 pre-K–5 students in a neighborhood with low socioeconomic status. The student population is 70% African American and Hispanic, and 90% of all students qualify for free or reduced lunch (Colorado Department of Education, 2006). Hunt staff implemented the academic component of RTI the first school year and added PBS the second year.

The staff adopted an RTI framework and formed professional learning communities. They aggressively improved teaching capacity in academics and behavior management. Student academic formative improvement data were posted on the wall in a "war room," while student behavioral data were reported regularly at staff meetings. The data below demonstrate the dramatic effect of the dual emphasis of an academic and behavior intervention plan after just 2 years of implementation (Brown, 2007).

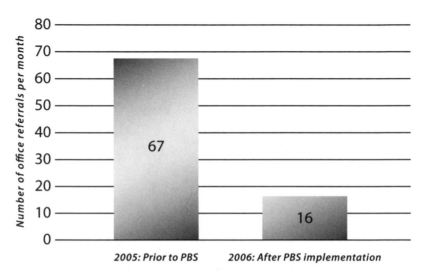

Before PBS: 67 referrals per month averaging 16 min. each = 160.2 hrs. of lost instruction time in 2005

After PBS: 16 referrals per month averaging 16 min. each = 37.8 hrs. of lost instruction time in 2006

PBS helped Hunt Elementary recover 122.4 hrs. of instruction.

Figure 4-2. Hunt Elementary Referral Rates Before and After Positive Behavior Support Implementation

From Brown, 2007. Used with permission.

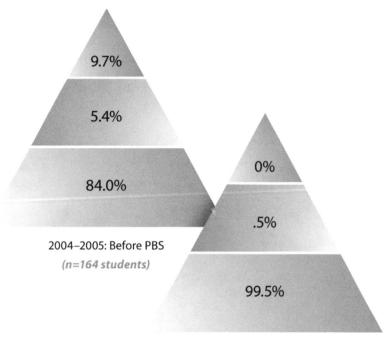

9.7%

5.4%

84.0%

2004–2005: Before PBS
(n=164 students)

0%

.5%

99.5%

2005–2006: After PBS
(n=184 students)

Figure 4-3. Percentages of Hunt Elementary Students at Each Tier in Reading, Before and After Positive Behavior Support Implementation

From Brown, 2007. Used with permission.

We are struck that the core principles of RTI implemented with fidelity transcend previously held beliefs that certain children, because of their minority status and economic situation, must perform poorly in school.

The next chapter will address progress monitoring as an efficient tool for gauging the effectiveness of instruction and determining whether instructional interventions are necessary. We will further look at the use of Problem-Solving Teams as the diagnostic and prescriptive entity to monitor student progress.

Chapter 5

Using Data

Progress monitoring provides the formative assessment link between instruction and high-stakes testing.

Progress Monitoring

The single most important error to avoid in setting up a Response to Intervention implementation plan is failing to provide school staff with in-depth, high-quality professional development and resources in progress monitoring—scientifically based tools and strategies to assess students' academic performance and evaluate effectiveness of instruction. The goal

goal should be to develop systemwide capacity in progress monitoring. Progress monitoring in an RTI initiative must include measures for districtwide progress, grade-level progress (K–12), schoolwide progress, classroom progress, and individual student progress. These measures *must* be aligned. The greatest problem is that many districts lack a truly aligned curriculum; aligned and linked curriculum ensures that what is taught is learned, and what is learned is measured. Districts with demonstrated success in reaching adequate yearly progress (AYP) are likely to have aligned curricula, while those failing to meet AYP do not. In addition, they most likely do not have valid and reliable formative and summative assessments.

No Child Left Behind, for better or worse, has placed emphasis on aligned curricula. In fact, districts with aligned curricula making AYP are rewarded, while those that do not and consequently fail to make AYP are sanctioned. We have discovered that unaligned curriculum and ineffective Tier 1 instruction create even more significant problems when combined. Districts generally should not wait to get curricula aligned and improve Tier 1 instruction prior to implementing RTI, because the stakes for students are too high. Students will continue to do poorly on high-stakes testing, and AYP will remain flat. A district in this position is in crisis, and crisis responses are necessary.

District leadership must set goals for the core curriculum to improve the horizontal and vertical alignment between classroom instructional expectations, grade-level requirements and standards, and assessments in math and language arts. In the past, much effort has been put into written curriculum standards and written assessments, with less attention given to the alignment of the instruction. Students are provided appropriate sequences and pacing in learning and sufficient review of learned skills and facts. They are then given numerous opportunities to apply skills and knowledge, in a variety of settings and with increased rigor in classes. The very name of academic departments (such as the math and the English departments) at secondary levels and district offices implies separation and lack of alignment across the curriculum. This departmentalization often leads to fragmentation and chaos in learning, versus systemic and systematic curriculum alignment. When students are faced with high-stakes testing appropriately aligned to standards and they do poorly, it is often a symptom of errors in the linkage of instruction (both vertically and horizontally), assessment, and the written curriculum. This requires a high degree of collaboration at all levels of instruction (K–12); there must be district leadership in aggressive approaches to eliminating what is not working (bad variables), and supporting that which is demonstrating results (good variables).

RTI creates curriculum alignment because of the heavy emphasis on progress monitoring. Progress monitoring puts into practice those questions asked in a professional learning community model: Are we teaching what students need to learn? Are the students learning what we teach? If not, what are we doing wrong, and what are we doing about it (DuFour, DuFour, & Eaker, 2005)?

The ultimate use of progress monitoring at a district level must include the analysis of high-stakes testing results over time and of formative district assessments (perhaps as frequently as every 3 weeks) aligned to standards assessed on high-stakes testing. In a professional learning community practicing RTI, results must be continuously monitored and analyzed, and the findings applied. This process leads to change in teacher and student learning and behavior.

One school district employing this PLC process is Aldine Independent School District in Houston, Texas. The district is home to 58,596 students, of whom 76% are eligible for the federal free and reduced lunch program. Just over 61% of the students are of Hispanic or Latino ethnicity, and 32% are African American. Twenty-eight percent of students qualify for English-language learner (ELL) instruction and 9% of students qualify for special education services (Aldine Independent School District, 2007). This district has a record of exceeding the state averages for all school districts. We observed a PLC in process at a large elementary school in Aldine ISD when data were received from the data management office on the same day a test was given.

Immediately, key staff went to work analyzing why one grade level performed poorly on a section of the math formative assessment. A call to central data management confirmed that other elementary school groups did well on the section—the assessment was valid and reliable—but this school did not. The "war room" went into overdrive, employing root cause analysis. The conclusion was that a section of the math assessment had been taught incorrectly, resulting in all students scoring poorly on the formative assessment. Within minutes, solutions were brought forward to correct the teaching errors.

Curriculum-Based Measurement

Curriculum-based measurements are quick, easy, normed assessments providing valuable clues on student learning.

Those students not progressing in basic skills must have even more discrete and sensitive measures provided more frequently. The National Center on Student Progress Monitoring (2007) has identified the following benefits of high-quality student progress monitoring:

- Accelerated learning due to students receiving more appropriate instruction

- More informed instructional decisions

- Documentation of student progress accountability purposes

- More efficient communication with families and other professionals about students' progress

- Higher expectations for students from teachers

- Fewer special education referrals

Most educational researchers agree that curriculum-based measurement (CBM) is helpful as individual, classroom, and district formative assessments (Deno, Espin, & Fuchs, 2002). *Curriculum-based measurements* are formative assessments that directly measure student performance within the existing curriculum. More specifically, according to the National Center on Student Progress Monitoring (2007), curriculum-based measurements:

- Assess a student's current functioning in the curriculum.

- Assist the RTI Problem-Solving Team in prescribing valid interventions.

- Establish instructional goals that work.

- Monitor progress in an aligned curriculum.

Most often, CBMs are used to measure the progress of student achievement in the basic skills of core academics— reading, writing, spelling, and math. However, with careful construction, CBMs can be created and normed for any curricular area.

CBMs are inexpensive, easy to use, and quickly administered in 2 to 5 minutes. An example of a CBM probe follows:

When using CBM to measure reading fluency, the examiner sits down individually with the child and has the student read aloud for 1 minute from each of three separate reading passages randomly chosen from a reading book. During the student's reading, the examiner makes note of any decoding errors made in each passage. Then the examiner calculates the number of words correctly read in the passage. Next, the examiner compares the word-totals correctly read for the three passages and chooses the middle, or median, score. This median score serves as the best indicator of the student's "true" reading rate in the selected reading material. (Wright, 2005, p. 7)

Probes enable teachers to monitor student progress on a daily, weekly, semimonthly, or monthly basis without loss of validity. Standardized instructions for administration and scoring support probe reliability. If instruction meets student needs, CBM data reveal progress. If instruction, for whatever reason, is not meeting student needs, outcome measures will be stagnant or decline.

Most critically, CBMs are sensitive to changes in individual student growth and in instructional methodology. Curriculum-based measurements help to do the following:

- Determine a student's individual instructional level within the curriculum.

- Establish long-term achievement goals, and monitor individuals and groups of students.

- Assist teachers and RTI Problem-Solving Teams in making decisions regarding the impact of teaching on learning.

- Measure the impact of interventions.

- Measure the impact of the overall RTI problem-solving process.

Many curriculum and instruction staff members have not been trained in curriculum-based measurements, and some may reject them offhand because they do not look like traditional ways to measure student progress. However, CBMs sample student performance quickly and easily give instant feedback to teachers. Consequently, they are the best tools for embedded root cause analysis.

One other value of CBMs was reflected in an actual incident at an elementary school in our district. Two students identified as "slow learners" (based on I.Q.) scored unsatisfactorily in reading on the state assessment. They were provided interventions in targeted reading skills and were assessed using DIBELS (Dynamic Indicators of Basic Early Literacy Skills) CBMs. Their teachers adjusted teaching based on the outcome data. At the end of the school year, one student scored proficient, and the other student performed at an advanced level in reading. Were these students slow learners? Probably not. They simply had missing skills or background knowledge. Bender and Shores (2007) report concerns that RTI may overidentify students with learning disabilities by eliminating exclusionary formulas and including large numbers of slow learners in the LD category. Others, including Fletcher and Reschly, report numbers of students at risk becoming functional readers when intervention is robust and early (Fletcher, Simos, Shaywitz, Shaywitz, Pugh, & Papanicolaou, 2000; Reschly, 2003).

Benchmarking

School districts are inundated with data, and too often staff members do not know what to do with it. Even when data abound, many districts have not worked out how to get the right data into the hands of teachers in a timely manner. Assessment and data interpretation are central to the Response to Intervention process. *Benchmarking* is the process of assessing all students three times per school year in reading, writing, and math. (As mentioned in chapter 4, in large secondary schools, particularly high schools, screening three times per year may be difficult. However, this cannot be an excuse to avoid measuring student performance. Students may be identified based on valid and reliable district assessments or the

Measures of Academic Progress [MAP] assessments, semiannual tests such as TerraNova, or the annual results of other high-stakes tests. Students below or significantly below proficient should be screened for baseline data.) Benchmarking is the first step in identifying students who are not benefiting from regular classroom instruction.

> High-quality professional development helps teachers move from understanding and using data to incorporating thoughtful, targeted assessments as part of the instructional process.

In an RTI system, progress monitoring is performed multiple times per year to ensure that students continue to progress adequately. If the data show that a student is not progressing, additional assessments may be administered more frequently to provide specific, up-to-date information. The RTI assessment process includes the following:

- Short tests (curriculum-based measurements, 2–3 minutes each) are administered to obtain baseline data on student skills.

- If a student learns at a slower rate or at a lower level than others in the classroom, the tests help the teacher pinpoint problems.

- The teacher changes teaching methods or materials so the student better understands the lessons, using progress monitoring assessments to track increased learning rates and alignment with student and class goals (Colorado Springs School District 11, 2006).

In Tier 1, data are required by the classroom teacher in order to make an accurate diagnosis of the performance of a student with learning problems in the general education classroom. A student referral may come from parents concerned about their child's performance; the classroom teacher may note a problem when analyzing one of the thrice-yearly benchmark data reports, or the referral may be a result of looking at student work. Let us take a look at the process of benchmarking.

Step 1: Median

Benchmark data should be supplemented with three or four curriculum-based measurement data points in order to accurately determine where a child is at that point in time. The median of these data points will determine the student's baseline (see Figure 5-1).

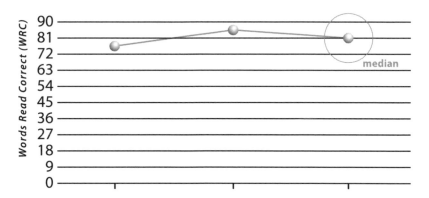

Figure 5-1. Student Benchmark Score for Reading

AIMSweb®. Copyright © 2007 by NCS Pearson, Inc. Reproduced with permission. All rights reserved. AIMSweb is a trademark, in the US and/or other countries, of Pearson Education, Inc. or its affiliate(s).

Step 2: Aim Line

Next, the teacher will determine where the student needs to be at a specific point in time: the aim or goal line. The trajectory between the baseline and the goal is the aim line for the student. The ordinate (y-axis) is performance, and the abscissa (x-axis) is time.

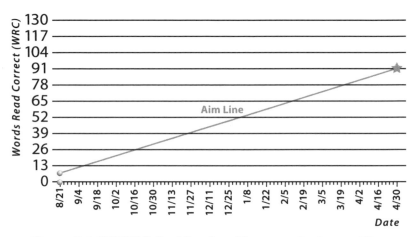

Figure 5-2. DIBELS Oral Reading Fluency—Student or Class Aim Line (Expected Rate of Progress: 2.30 WRC per Week)

Step 3: Trend Line

The trend line is the result of plotting periodic progress monitoring data points garnered from the interventions used with the student to remove the learning problem.

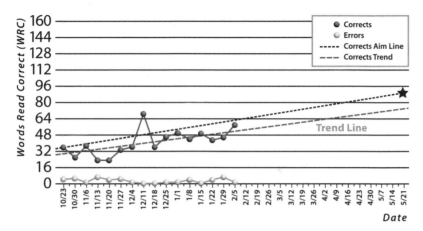

Figure 5-3. Grade 1 Reading—Student Data Trend Line (Standard Progress Monitoring Passages)

AIMSweb®. Copyright © 2007 by NCS Pearson, Inc. Reproduced with permission. All rights reserved. AIMSweb is a trademark, in the US and/or other countries, of Pearson Education, Inc. or its affiliate(s).

Step 4: Trend Data

The final step is to analyze the trend data to determine if the interventions are successfully addressing the student's learning problem or if a change should be made. If the slope of the trend line is less than the slope of the aim line, then the results are less than expected, and a change should be made in the intervention or to its intensity. If the slope of the trend line is significantly greater than the slope of the aim line, then the aim line may be too low. If the slope of the two lines is similar, then the intervention is working, and no changes should be made.

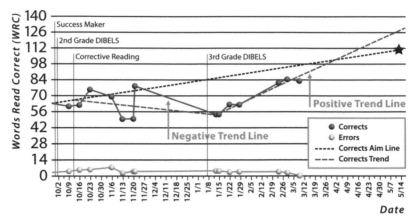

**Figure 5-4. Grade 3: DIBELS Oral Reading Fluency
(Examples of Negative and Positive Trend Lines)**

*AIMSweb®. Copyright © 2007 by NCS Pearson, Inc. Reproduced with
permission. All rights reserved. AIMSweb is a trademark, in the US and/or
other countries, of Pearson Education, Inc. or its affiliate(s).*

Graphing Student Data in Problem-Solving Teams

In Tier 2, the same process for determining the baseline
performance of the student—charting the aim line and plotting the trend—is used by the Problem-Solving Team for
students requiring more targeted supplemental instruction
than can be provided in the general education classroom. The
frequency of progress monitoring data points may increase, as
may the frequency, intensity, and duration of the interventions,
which may occur in the classroom or another setting. Based
on data, a small percentage (5–10%) of students may require
more explicit, more intensive help, in some cases specifically
designed Tier 3 instruction, to meet their learning needs
(Fletcher, Fuchs, Lyon, & Barnes, 2006; Foorman, 2003;
Fuchs, Fuchs, & Compton, 2003; Gresham, 1991; Reschly,
2003; Tilly, 2003). This may or may not include referral to
special education.

We strongly recommend the use of an electronic data management system to allow the classroom teacher and the PSTs to graph student data without that component becoming an overwhelming factor and impeding the total RTI process. Data can be graphed using a spreadsheet, though this may be labor-intensive. Use the following directions to create trend lines in Microsoft® Office Excel 2002:

1. Enter student data (such as number of words read correctly and number of errors).

WEEK	WORDS CORRECT/ MINUTE	ERRORS/MINUTE
1	12	1
2	22	2
3	34	5
4	45	4
5	47	5
6	49	3
7	52	3
8	66	2

Figure 5-5. Example of Student Data

2. Using the Chart Wizard, create a "line" graph.

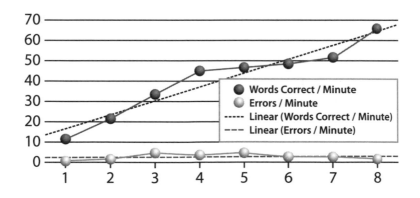

Figure 5-6. Example Line Graph Created From Student Data

3. On the graph, click on the line to which you would like to add a trend line.

4. Go to the "chart" tab (hold down the mouse button until all options are displayed).

5. Click on "Add trend line."

6. Click on "linear."

7. Click "OK."

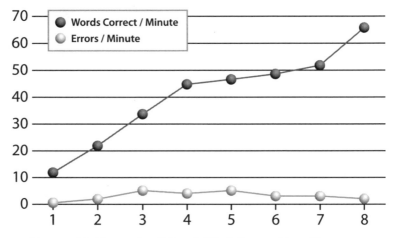

Figure 5-7. Example of Graph With Linear Trend Line

At the time of publication, the commercial assessment system we feel best meets the requirements for probes, data tracking, and graphing is AIMSweb®. Information is available at www.aimsweb.com.

As a district builds its data systems to align with curriculum and instruction, leadership must ensure that resources are in place to support classrooms and schools. Furthermore, progress monitoring must be ongoing, including weekly Tier 2 and Tier 3 assessments, monthly and quarterly Tier 1 assessments, thrice-annual benchmarking, and annual high-stakes testing. Aligned systemic assessments foster aligned screening, benchmarking, diagnosis, and intervention.

One of the most exciting uses of data is the ability to show parents how and why their student is progressing. Parents (and students) are often frustrated by letter or number grades because they provide little information on what is successful, and what needs to improve. Teachers who graphically demonstrate student progress and how progress relates to specific interventions create the basis for lively and positive dialogue with parents. Parent involvement, as discussed in the next chapter, is an integral part of the RTI process.

Chapter 6
Parent Involvement

In a perfect world, all children have equal gifts. In a perfect world, all children are healthy and happy. It is not a perfect world. Children need an array of skills, high expectations, and support to be successful. Parents can be Response to Intervention's greatest ally in this endeavor.

Parents can be challenging. Schools hear from parents who are opinionated, vocal, and determined; schools usually do not hear from parents who are disenfranchised, scared, or indifferent. Both are frustrating. What educators and parents have in common is a desire for children to be successful. While parents are not the educators during the school day, they are the educators during the remaining 16 hours spent at home and in the community. At the district and school levels, an RTI framework must value parent input and engagement. (Throughout this chapter, the word *parent* implies any caring adult—parent, grandparent, aunt, uncle, or guardian—with a child in the school system who is impacted by Response to Intervention.)

Ruby Payne's (2003) work on poverty and education acknowledges that public school is a middle-class construct. It uses middle-class language, norms, and expectations. School language, expectations, requirements, and structures impose barriers on those who:

- Lack financial resources
- Are non-English speakers
- Have low literacy or education levels
- Lack comfort in a school setting
- Lack educational systems' expertise and language
- Receive negative messages about their child consistently

Schools must decrease these and other barriers to fully engage parents in education. In an RTI system, parents can help complete a holistic picture of a student within the context of school, family, and community. Parents can provide support and continuity of academic and behavioral interventions, as well as grassroots support for systemic educational change. RTI provides an avenue for welcoming and valuing parents' unique perspectives.

Parent Involvement in the District Round Table

Creating a shared RTI vision and common language includes parent involvement on the District Round Table. Parent involvement is a four-step process:

1. Identification and recruitment

2. Professional development

3. Team meeting logistics

4. Opportunities for contribution

Identification and Recruitment

Identifying and recruiting parents to the District Round Table may be easy or difficult depending on the size and demographics of the district and its history of parent inclusion. While it is impossible to include representatives from all constituencies, the Round Table Team benefits from having parents who represent both elementary and secondary levels. The goal is to build a collaborative relationship through multiple voices.

Recruitment should delineate the rationale for implemen-ting RTI to parents, as well as the goals for the Round Table and an outline of Round Table Team member roles, responsibilities, and time commitments. Look for parents who are experienced advocates, comfortable with discussing issues with school and district staff; for less-experienced parents, the Round Table can be intimidating and counterproductive. Parents of struggling learners are ideal candidates for recruitment. They understand how students become disenfranchised and disconnected from learning, and are usually anxious for systemic improvement and willing to actively participate over several years.

Professional Development

Round Table parents and staff both benefit from professional development, which provides common understanding and common language. Professional development may be offered to Round Table members only or can be expanded to include school-based teams. Ideal are presentations by experts on:

- The foundations of RTI
- Research-based interventions
- Short-term assessments
- Data management

Additional discussions with schools or districts that have successfully implemented RTI provide a "heads up" about potential problems and solution options. Parents included in professional development can become active, knowledgeable participants in the RTI root cause analysis process, advocates for RTI implementation, and connectors to key parent communicators in the schools and in the community.

Team Meeting Logistics

Team meeting logistics become critical to active parent participation. The District Round Table should:

- Establish meeting times and expectations that do not unequally burden parents. This may include holding meetings when everyone is on "volunteer time."
- Ensure productive meetings with agendas, overviews of the work to be accomplished, task assignments, and opportunities for questions and discussion.
- Adhere to meeting times; start and end on time. All members appreciate consistency, and this facilitates childcare and scheduling for staff and parents.

- Adhere to the norm that confines discussions to school and district systems, not to individual teachers or students. Meetings tend to veer off course when individual issues rule discussions. This is a particular pitfall for parents who come from a narrower perspective than district- and school-level educators. Refocusing team members on critical issues and system gaps moves the design and decision-making processes forward without discounting individual contributions. It should be noted that using an external facilitator may diminish power struggles and potential animosity.

Opportunities for Contribution

Finally, parents want to contribute and know their efforts lead to positive change. As Round Table Team members, parents will participate in root cause analysis (see chapter 3). This may provide key opportunities for a parent and staff member to make RTI overview presentations to district accountability groups, parent teacher associations or parent teacher organizations (PTAs or PTOs), or district advisory councils. Presentations can generate RTI awareness and garner input from a broader parent constituency on district issues and gaps. RTI subcommittees can provide opportunities for a diverse mix of parents to tackle specific RTI supports, such as parent communication, training, and supplementary printed materials. The district can support schools by developing:

- An RTI program website
- A list of frequently asked questions (see appendix D, page 179, for examples).
- Information for the district cable or television network, if available, or other district communication vehicles
- A series of "RTI Basics" articles for school newsletters

- A DVD or PowerPoint on RTI basics for open houses and school events

As RTI implementation progresses, parents and other Round Table members can provide information talks at school accountability and PTA or PTO meetings. Districtwide meetings can be highly effective when combined with an RTI guest expert (either nationally recognized or from an experienced district).

Rollout Plan

Providing parents with too much information too early can result in backlash from parents and staff. Parents may ask questions that staff cannot answer, and may want immediate RTI implementation and results. Staff may become defensive because they do not yet have the knowledge or expertise to respond to parent demands. Staff and administrators at all levels first need a foundational understanding of RTI, and they also appreciate seeing parent information materials prior to their distribution.

Districts benefit from an RTI rollout plan to train groups of schools as they exhibit key readiness indicators. A similar rollout plan for parent information and education is beneficial; key components include development of RTI materials and short training sessions for all school staff, district-level administrators, and key building communicators such as the PTA or PTO.

Parent Inclusion

Dauber and Epstein (1991) found that many parents respond to encouragement from educators. In their national study of 2,317 inner-city elementary and middle school students, the best predictor of parent involvement was what the school did to promote it. School attitudes and actions were more important than the parents' income, education level, race, or previous school-volunteering experience in predicting whether a parent would be involved in the school. Parent involvement is more diverse at the school level than the district level and has three main components: planning, informing, and involving.

> Create a parent inclusion plan that melds education, parenting, and public relations.

Planning

As planners, parents are members of the RTI School Leadership Team and the School Behavioral Leadership Team. These teams may be the same or separate depending on the size of the school. (The School Behavioral Team will be present in schools implementing Positive Behavior Support or other schoolwide behavioral models. In small schools, the RTI Leadership and Behavioral Leadership Teams may be one and the same.) A School Behavioral Leadership Team uses the strategies for developing root cause solutions to off-task student behaviors. Typical members could include the principal, a bus driver, lunchroom staff, a gym teacher, classroom teachers, or safety coordinators. These teams use data from behavioral incidents just as the academic teams use achievement data to identify cause and effect relationships to improve the educational environment. Recruitment from various grade levels and constituent groups is optimal. Professional development on RTI builds a common foundation between all team members. All team members help develop the schoolwide RTI implementation plan. In particular, parents should guide planning and product development for the parent communication process and provide input on how best to involve parents in Problem-Solving Teams.

Informing

Informing parents means effectively conveying the essential concepts of RTI and their impact to the various groups within the school. Examples of such groups include the PTA or PTO, Title I parent representatives, special education support groups, booster clubs, and special project constituents (for example, a curriculum reform group). Although when, where, and how schools inform parents about RTI is unique to each site, an information process incorporates the basic concepts of public relations in the following five steps.

Step 1: Define the Issue

Who are the target audiences?

- All parents
- Low-literacy or non-English-speaking parents
- Special education parents

What do they need to know?

- What Response to Intervention is
- How it will impact the classroom
- How it will impact individual students

Step 2: Establish Objectives

What do we want to accomplish, and how will we measure success?

- General RTI information
    - Number of messages provided
    - Number of parents impacted
- Participation in parent-student-teacher dialogues
    - Parents' understanding of progress monitoring data
- Active participation in the problem-solving process

- Parents' understanding of short-term assessments and progress monitoring goals, and support of student action planning

Step 3: Establish Strategies

What should we do and say, and why? When and how do we say it?

- Strategy 1
    - Who: All parents
    - Why: RTI overview for general information
    - How: A PowerPoint presentation
    - When: Open House
- Strategy 2
    - Who: Spanish-speaking parents
    - Why: Increase ability to understand data in parent-teacher conferences
    - How: Small group presentations with data using the bilingual community liaison
    - When:
    a) 20 minutes prior to band and choir performances
    b) A session in a Title I parent meeting
    c) Workshop rotation at the school literacy night

Step 4: Create a Public Relations Plan

What are the tasks to accomplish our strategies?

- Identify the key components of each strategy.
- Identify the resources to develop each component—people, funds, materials, location, and communication and outreach.
- Identify who is responsible for project components.
- Identify the timeline for completion.

- Identify how data will be collected to gauge impact.

Step 5: Evaluate

How did we do?

- How does the outcome data compare with the objectives?
- How can we do a better job next time?

With any public relations (PR) campaign, the key is to establish multiple layers of information. An advertising maxim states that people need to get the information 7 to 11 times before it becomes part of their awareness. To help ensure RTI buy-in and participation, repeat the message in a variety of ways so it connects with visual, spatial, auditory, and kinesthetic learners.

One final PR note: Every school has key parent influencers and communicators. These individuals drive the people-to-people network within the school and community. It is important to include them in key training, brainstorming, and planning sessions; this gets the word out to all parents quickly and inexpensively.

Involving

Parental involvement is the crux of a collaborative school-home partnership. Problem-Solving Teams can be highly effective in identifying learning issues, creating a data-based action plan, and supporting tiered interventions (see chapter 3). PSTs can operate without a parent component, but when the parent is added as an equal team member, student outcomes are strengthened.

In contrast to special education child study teams, parents and PST members focus on current home, student motivation, and student performance data. The most effective PSTs develop a multistep parent involvement process:

1. **Engage parents in conversation** *before* **the PST meeting.** Students receiving Tier 1 classroom interventions need support from home. Assignment folders, phone calls, notes home, and quick conversations in the hallway help connect parents to current learning issues.

2. **For Tier 1 and Tier 2 students, establish a process for obtaining the parental perspective on student assets and challenges.** A standard parent survey form is often used (see appendix C, page 177). It can be mailed, emailed, delivered by hand, or discussed by phone. The survey allows the parent to not only contribute valuable information, but also to begin thinking about the child's learning issues *prior* to the PST meeting.

3. **Provide parents with a realistic expectation of the PST process.** Identify the time and format of the meeting, who will be there, the meeting goal, and expectations for the parent. To help the parent overcome fear of interaction with educational professionals, allow him or her to invite a relative, the community liaison, or a close friend.

4. **Create a welcoming atmosphere.** Emphasize student strengths during the problem-solving process. Many parents hear only what their child cannot or does not accomplish, and they crave hearing how his or her assets can help to overcome challenges. A welcoming atmosphere also increases the likelihood the parent will stay involved.

5. **Use data, not opinions, to identify issues and establish expectations.** This removes accusations of personality conflict and focuses on measurable outcomes. Parents, students, and teachers have concrete evidence of what needs to be accomplished.

6. **Incorporate specific home-based strategies that can support student goals.** Development of these strate-

gies should be a collaborative effort; strategies should be within the parent's ability to achieve.

7. **Provide regular feedback on student progress.** Update goals and strategies as needed.

Parent involvement at any level increases when barriers decrease. Potential issues around language, transportation, meeting logistics, childcare, and literacy must be minimized if parents are to be active RTI participants.

> **Y**ou are the experts in understanding your community, the issues, and the supports necessary for parent participation. Be creative.

Schools can be very creative in involving parents. Schools can create parent packets, in various languages, that include:

- A general RTI brochure or flyer
- Information on the various interventions included in the school's unique RTI program
- Explanation of how RTI impacts students, classrooms, parents, teachers, and the school
- A list of school and district resources

Some schools hold mock Problem-Solving Team meetings so parents and students may understand the process better. An RTI information table can be available at an open house in middle schools and high schools. Teachers can post classroom data, trend lines, and aim lines in the hallway so parents and students learn the common data language. A high school counselor may meet parents at a local coffee shop after work to discuss student progress and challenges. An elementary school can begin each day 10 minutes early to incorporate a school-wide assembly, where staff deliver an RTI-based behavioral skills lesson, school announcements, and RTI outcomes, and also present academic progress awards. Parents can bring their children and stay for the 10-minute daily jumpstart, keeping them informed and involved. The key for your school is to identify the parent, school, and neighborhood needs and create the parent engagement strategies that meet those needs.

What Happens When Parents Experience the Success of Response to Intervention?

Once, a highly frustrated parent contacted the director of special education in the same district where we were developing RTI systems. Her student, Charlie, was in her freshman year in high school, and the year was not going well. Charlie had been identified as having dyslexia by a private practitioner and had qualified for special education in elementary school. In middle school, Charlie improved her reading yet still read at elementary level (2 years below grade level), but no longer met the criteria for having a learning disability under the discrepancy formula. She was dropped from special education and reading support services for most of her middle school years. Charlie made little progress in reading but was promoted through the grades anyway.

Retested at the high school level, Charlie once again met criteria for special education services. However, this frustrated freshman was failing classes, getting discouraged, and developing negative behavior patterns. Her mother was introduced to the RTI concept. She agreed to a strategic reading intervention program involving in-school tutoring (the services had to be imported because the high school lacked highly trained literacy intervention staff).

During tutoring, a special education teacher became interested in a strategic and structured reading intervention, and was later trained for it. The reading intervention was multisensory and incorporated structured practice with immediate, corrective feedback to develop automatic word recognition skills.

The intervention program was expanded, by the tutor and the special educator, to include other students with similar disabilities. The outcome, after one semester, revealed that all eight program students demonstrated significant improvement over students attending general English classes and off-the-shelf intervention programs—more than 1 year's growth in one semester of intervention.

Charlie continued with the strategic reading intervention over the next 3 years. She was ultimately reassessed in reading skills using standard protocols, and tested proficient and above grade level in reading comprehension when she graduated from high school. Her mother became an advocate for RTI and spoke passionately at a public meeting and to the board of education in support of its continued implementation.

Parents and schools that have embraced a collegial and inclusive atmosphere will find it easier to meld RTI and special education practices. As illustrated in the next chapter, parents of special education students have been highly receptive to the differentiated and targeted instruction their child receives in an RTI framework. When implemented with fidelity, RTI accelerates learning for special education students, rather than just providing additional services.

Chapter 7

Special Education and RTI

> RTI expands the possibilities for special education. To do this, it requires strong leadership, risk-taking, and up-to-date, high-quality instruction.

Moving From Discrepancy Formulas

A strong impetus for RTI on a national basis has been the change in IDEA (2004) making discrepancy formulas optional for school districts. In the past, special educators used the discrepancy formulas to determine student eligibility. It is generally accepted nationally that about 10% of a student body might have significant disabilities that require special education intervention. Within this group of students, it is not unusual to find 60% of those students qualifying for learning disabilities services. To qualify these students, special educators used a discrepancy formula that identified a mostly arbitrary difference between the students' academic progress and their intelligence quotients (I.Q.), particularly for learning disability services.

The new IDEA stance of permissive use of discrepancy formulas may seem benign. It is not. Discrepancy formulas will essentially need to be abandoned as states and districts that use them will be fighting and losing battles against special education legal advocates in due process hearings. Advocates will use high-quality research findings to demonstrate that the formulas do not work, to identify and to exclude students from services. Although not intended to do so, the formulas made it appear easy to identify students with learning disabilities by eliminating root cause problem identification from the eligibility determination process. Staff did not have to struggle with the root causes of low student performance. A student either met or did not meet the formula, and this process alone served as a district's special education determination. Hence came the phrase *waiting for students to fail*—districts waited for a student to fail before offering the intervention the student required to be successful. As states and districts migrate into the RTI process and away from a stringent discrepancy formula, several key issues need to be addressed: core curriculum fidelity, resource alignment, commitment to professional learning communities, and changes in role definition and staff capacity.

Core Curriculum Fidelity

A rule of thumb is that if 80% of students are not performing at or above proficiency levels, then universal core instruction is not working adequately. RTI requires core instruction and curriculum to provide a strong foundation in math and literacy skills (at least). If this does not occur, the numbers of students placed into Tier 2 and 3 interventions will overwhelm school systems and create a disproportionate number of students in strategic and intensive services. More importantly, students will be failing not because of innate lack of ability to learn, but because of instructional deficits.

Resource Alignment

Once all students requiring interventions are embraced, staff must share talents and funding if the entire learning community is to support all students in need. However, district leaders are often concerned that as they become more proficient in RTI implementation, special education numbers will decrease. Because most federal and state program funding is tied to numbers of identified students, districts will be required to do more with less. For this reason, states must begin the process of collaboration at the federal and local levels to ensure that funding is not reduced for services that *prevent* overidentification of learning disabilities identification and improve student achievement.

Commitment to Professional Learning Communities

When a school makes a commitment to become a professional learning community, a shared vision coordinates planning time, inspires collegial collaboration, and generates enthusiasm for meeting individual goals for all students. PLCs present both a procedural and cultural change for most districts and schools. Whenever school districts and schools have moved from underperforming to meeting high standards, leadership has clearly modeled this change and held everyone equally accountable.

Changes in Role Definition and Staff Capacity

Under the discrepancy formula, school psychologists used the data from psychoeducational assessments to determine special education eligibility. However, the impact on student interventions was not restricted to school psychologists. At special education staffing meetings, general education teachers had to fight for their students to receive special services. Special education service providers worked to ensure that students requiring general classroom interventions (rather than special education) did not overwhelm their caseloads, and parents formed troops of special education advocates to watch the battle and cheer for more student services to be written into individualized education programs.

It is not enough to just change the roles of individuals in RTI. Carefully designed professional development is required to restructure roles, modify expectations, and build internal capacity. Failure to do so will result in staff and parents functioning in the old way. The new way of decision-making will be based on uncovering and repairing root causes of student underachievement prior to determining special education eligibility, particularly for learning disability qualification.

Additional legal issues need to be addressed by school districts under RTI, as the following quote illustrates:

> In using an RTI process a district may have to defend a parental claim that a district has failed to refer and evaluate a student in a timely manner. A district in such a case, and other cases, will need to defend its RTI process legally. In Upper Darby School District, [106 LRP 60495 - PA SEA 2006], the hearing officer found the district's RTI system inadequate:
>
> > "The record shows that the psychologist did a records review, administered some standardized testing, and reviewed the [evaluation] materials concluding that

Student had no learning disability. This process falls short of the requirements for a response to intervention determination. Most importantly, the district conducted no intervention, collected no data, and did not examine students' response to intervention in the area previously identified as a learning disability. Thus, the District can determine neither whether the Student continues to meet the criteria for identification as a student with a specific learning disability (SLD), nor can it determine if any interventions are effective. The District's evaluation report is fatally flawed in that it did not follow the prescribed protocol for an RTI process." (Gallegos, 2007, p. 5)

RTI expands options for special education, *but only when implemented with fidelity.*

Schools and school districts must be well-prepared to leave the discrepancy model behind.

Moving From Discrepancy-Based Formulas

We acquired information about the current national trends on RTI through networking with other RTI implementers, reading newsletters of related fields, and networking at national conferences (such as the Association for Supervision and Curriculum Development, Education Trust, and American Association of School Administrators) with educational researchers (for example, Reschly, Tilly, Fletcher, and Foorman) and school district attorneys focused on special education. RTI is so new that the legal interpretations and impact on special education are still being developed. In special education, outcomes of due process hearings and appeals in appellate courts tend to interpret and drive how districts invoke due process and practice. We believe that logic and common sense should precede the development of formalized state and district policies and procedures. Otherwise, rules may hamper educators' attempts to meet the strong values of RTI—early intervention and progress monitoring—prior to identification of eligibility for special education. The following steps are critical for implementation of RTI with fidelity as an integrated practice:

1. Communicate thoroughly and regularly with all stakeholders, including parents, teachers, administrators, and community activists about the benefits of RTI compared to traditional methods of identification.

2. Phase out the discrepancy formula based on a school's measured capacity to use RTI with fidelity in identification of special education students.

3. Do not force RTI if conflict arises. Some students, staff, and parents will benefit from seeing the progress students make, using the discrepancy formula as a baseline. Provide dual systems for some students, if necessary.

4. Do not talk about "RTI kids" or "putting students in RTI." RTI is a process, not a place or a label.

5. Continually share, under guidelines of confidentiality, the successes of individual students in RTI.

6. Evaluate and share districtwide success in closing achievement gaps.

7. Continually provide professional development across the school system in preservice and in-service events to ensure that RTI is perceived as a general education function impacting *all* students, regardless of labels.

In our district, guidelines established during initial RTI development in 2005 have resulted in zero mediations, zero due process hearings, and zero complaints filed based on RTI practices. The U.S. Department of Education, in its discussion of 34 C.F.R. §300.309, states, "Well-implemented RTI models and models that identify problems early and promote intervention have reduced, not increased, the number of children identified as eligible for special education services and have helped raise achievement levels for all children in a school" (Gallegos, 2007, p. 7).

Intervention in lieu of the discrepancy formula provides more options for special education students and students with learning disabilities.

Questions and Concerns

The following questions and concerns surface frequently as districts move from discrepancy formulas to an RTI framework: Are we screening or evaluating? Can we refuse a referral to special education while a student is in the RTI process?

Are We Screening or Evaluating?

RTI requires screening through benchmark assessments, progress monitoring, and reviews of student records. IDEA 2004 (Individuals with Disabilities Education Act) has clarified that screening is not considered an evaluation for eligibility in special education and related services. Consequently, parental consent is not required for screening (Individuals with Disabilities Education Improvement Act, 2004).

Can We Refuse a Referral to Special Education?

If the Problem-Solving Team feels the referral is premature, the district may refuse to evaluate and continue the RTI process as a screening process. However, districts need to be sure to provide the appropriate prior written notice and procedural safeguards to parents. It is important to collaborate with parents and assist them in understanding the RTI process and its benefits to their child. In an informal survey with other district special education directors, most districts implementing RTI with fidelity have reported that they have received no parental complaints during or after implementation. School districts and state departments of education must be sure they are continually aligning the RTI process to both IDEA 2004 and state rules and regulations.

Certification

Schools must become excellent communicators about the RTI process, why it is being used, and what it means for student progress in academics and behavior. It is recommended that schools be "certified" by their school district director of special education to move from a discrepancy model to an RTI model. The certification must be based on objective capacity and readiness criteria for instituting RTI as a step in special education identification and eligibility. It is helpful for the district to create a logic model and strategic plan (see appendix B, pages 162–163) delineating the implementation and evaluation objectives and benchmarks.

Quantifying RTI Resource Levels

Quantifying current special and general education resource levels in RTI includes program or intervention validity in current settings, use of time by specialists, specialist capacity, and budget allocations for testing and assessments that are no longer required. Districts that have analyzed these issues have come to some of the following conclusions:

1. Specialty staff requires continuous professional development, monitoring, and feedback in using curriculum-based measurements, monitoring progress, interpreting

assessments to provide and support interventions, using Problem-Solving Teams, and implementing professional learning communities. Additional professional development, monitoring, and feedback are necessary to improve instructional knowledge of strategic reading and math skills development.

2. Classroom teachers and special educators should be cotrained in differentiated instruction and provided with coaching opportunities.

3. Choices of curriculum materials should be drastically narrowed to the key programs that will create results in core academics and intervention instruction.

4. Silos of service delivery should be eliminated to improve service efficiency, prevent duplication, and increase flexible resource utilization.

5. Eliminating traditional testing practices will increase time availability of specialists for collaboration with all staff and direct intervention with students.

6. The use of Problem-Solving Teams will drastically reduce time in special education staffings, as student needs will be met prior to referral to special education and data will already have been collected for students requiring referrals.

Changes in staff roles and capacities require strategic planning. Most professionals embrace RTI as a method of improving student achievement and enriching the job satisfaction of educators. Some staff will participate willingly, some hesitantly, and some will not take part at all. District and school leaders must effectively manage all reactions to change. Job descriptions must reflect new role expectations. Support must be provided in coaching. Progress monitoring and outcome accountability should be provided in a continuous quality improvement management process delivering feedback to all.

RTI involves educational redesign at all levels of the organization. As with all educational endeavors, RTI requires state-of-the-art instruction, leadership, and risk-taking to ensure that the initiative takes hold, demonstrates success, and is sustained.

Chapter 8

Evaluation

Evaluation empowers decision-making. It begins with determining root causes or issues contributing to the success or failure of RTI in the areas of leadership, management, curriculum, instruction, and assessment.

We conducted extensive research on RTI and discovered that little evaluation or research exists on the efficacy of RTI as a system designed to improve student achievement, particularly when implemented across an entire school district. Research does exist on the high positive correlation between early intervention and student achievement (Foorman, 2003; Scanlon, Vellutino, Small, Fanuele, & Sweeney, 2003; Torgesen, 2000; Torgesen, Rose, Lindamood, Conway, & Garvan, 1999; Vellutino, Scanlon, Sipay, Small, Pratt, Chen, & Denckla, 1996). However, we needed to know if and how RTI functions systemically. What constitutes the measurement of RTI as successful or unsuccessful? What facilitates success of RTI in systems, and what inhibits it? What are the pitfalls and assets to RTI development, particularly in large school districts? This chapter addresses four areas of evaluation and research: 1) student outcomes, 2) consumer acceptability, 3) systems change, and 4) fidelity of systemic RTI implementation. Data on progress in each area are provided, with particular focus on student achievement and systems change. We present some initial findings at the end of the chapter, with cautions and recommendations to leaders of RTI in schools, districts, and state offices of education. Our findings represent only a small sampling of what is possible to attain and the types of data a district might want to capture.

Implementation across a district or within a school setting without a strong evaluation plan is a predictor of failure for RTI as a sustainable reform process. We have experience with several systems where the RTI initiative has been attempted without strategic planning or a built-in evaluation plan. These systems floundered and allowed variables for failure. Examples of missteps in real schools, districts, and state offices we know of include:

- Inadequate resource planning for the strategic implementation of school, district, or statewide change

- Failure to garner sufficient leadership support and understanding of the full breadth and depth of RTI from key stakeholders

- Failure to plan for the professional development of administrators, staff, and parents

- Failure to identify and address barriers to achievement reform in the district (to perform root cause analysis)

- Failure to plan for and develop an adequate data management system and assessment instruments to provide baseline and progress monitoring of student performance

Appropriate evaluation of RTI does not judge right or wrong, good or bad. Evaluation empowers better decision-making. Moreover, evaluation is not about statistics alone; it is about discovering root causes of variables leading to success and failure. Ultimately, evaluation focuses on asking the right questions.

The Evaluation Process

Evaluation begins with assessing root causes or issues determining success or failure of RTI in five areas: leadership, management, curriculum, instruction, and assessment or evaluation. Notice that management is distinct from leadership. Leadership provides the vision and direction; management carries out the vision. Effective RTI management requires district and school leadership to identify root causes *before* designing RTI implementation and evaluation. (This process is presented in more detail in chapter 9.)

Once the root causes for success or failure are identified, the system should create SMART goals—strategic and specific, measurable, attainable, results-based, and time-bound (O'Neill & Conzemius, 2006)—or measurable objectives that support continuous quality improvement. The objectives create measurable end points that should be achievable if the negative root cause is diminished or eliminated. For example:

- Root cause—Students lack the reading comprehension skills to achieve proficiency in language arts.

- Measurable objective—By April 2008, at least 80% of all students in grades 3–10 will score at least at the proficient level on the state-sanctioned assessment exam in literacy.

The district or school should then choose one or more strategies, such as RTI, for achieving the objective. The evaluation process then begins by asking questions. For example:

1. What instructional changes will cause the greatest positive impact on student achievement with the fewest resources?

2. Which group of instructional strategies is most effective for students in middle school who are at least 2 years behind grade level in their reading comprehension?

3. How effective are RTI Problem-Solving Teams in identifying appropriate interventions based on student data?

4. Is the curriculum effective with Tier 1 students when delivered with fidelity?

In this example, not all questions can be answered, particularly in year-one implementation. However, district and school leadership should determine which questions are most relevant to short- and long-term decision-making and include them in the evaluation process.

The next step is to identify the type of data necessary to answer the questions. Data are generally one of three types. *Output data* count things or actions, such as the number of students served, percentage of students in each tier of instruction, frequency of PST meetings, or number of teachers receiving RTI training. Outputs are valuable quantifiers of how the RTI project was implemented and who was impacted. In contrast, *outcome data* denote change; data answer questions about how the target audience—students, teachers— was impacted by RTI implementation. Outcome data include changes in achievement, learning rates, percent of movement between tiers, teacher competency for delivering interventions with fidelity, or changes in the number of students referred for further interventions. The third type of data is *efficiency indicators*. These data express how resources were used to produce x benefit for y cost. Efficiency indicators help quantify resource utilization for students, gauge the impact of student gains against program costs, and provide the basis for sustainability planning.

The subsequent evaluation steps are those traditionally quantified as the "evaluation process": delineating the data collection framework and tools, and establishing an action plan—who, what, when, where—for data collection. The steps are relatively simple, and the extent of the data collection process is often based on or constricted by district and school resources. Leaders should be creative about how to obtain the data needed. Evaluators can be efficient by taking advantage of teacher satisfaction surveys and adding a few key questions that address RTI. Quality management systems may use periodic checklists or principal observation data for implementation fidelity (quantified walkthroughs of intervention programming), and analyze student work on a regular basis. District and state specialists can be invaluable in creating surveys and aggregating data from central student-assessment systems. Together, theses sources can create a rich body of evidence on RTI efficacy.

Final evaluation steps include data analysis, conclusions, recommendations, and reporting. Analysis examines outputs, outcomes, and efficiency indicators. It also looks for trends and key insights. Questioning is imperative, for example:

- What did we discover?
- How effective were we in creating the desired change?
- How should the program be modified or improved?
- What are the implications for sustainability?

- What are the implications for replication?

Conclusions and recommendations should be presented at least biannually. It is helpful to examine key data midway through implementation. This formative data may lead to a valuable midcourse correction that significantly impacts summative data. In presenting analysis and data, managers should build a case for program continuation and sustainability. RTI leaders can use these data to outline key needs and issues, why strategies were chosen, what participants hoped to accomplish, what was implemented, what the data show, and current and future impact on the measurable objectives. The logic model in Figure 8-1 presents the evaluation process visually.

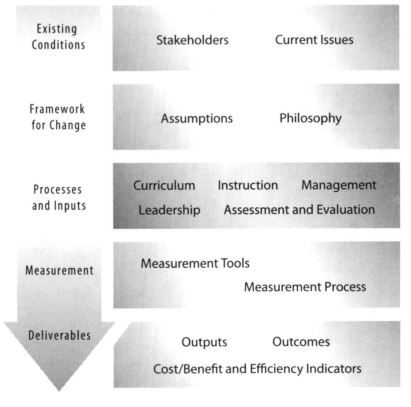

Figure 8-1. Sample Logic Model: Response to Intervention Evaluation Process

Key Categories of Evaluation

A convenient way of quantifying the evaluation process is to examine four categories: student outcomes, consumer acceptability, systems change, and implementation fidelity.

Dan Reschly (2005, personal correspondence) of Vanderbilt University has outlined four key categories for structuring RTI evaluation: 1) student outcomes, 2) consumer acceptability, 3) systems change, and 4) implementation fidelity. These four strategies form the basis for the evaluation process. Throughout our work with various school districts, most evaluation questions about leadership, management, curriculum, and instruction could be captured within these categories.

Student Outcomes

Student outcomes are the most obvious evaluation category—the culmination of the RTI system impact. A management system such as AIMSweb® facilitates benchmarking and progress monitoring data on individual students, groups of students, classrooms, grade levels, schools, and the district as a whole. Differentiating between achievement and rate of improvement is critical. Students most significantly behind their peers may take several years to catch up, and their achievement data may reveal little gross progress. However, examining improvement in raw scores is helpful. Even more critical is the rate of improvement. If Tier 2 and Tier 3 students make 2 or more years of gain in a year, they are closing the achievement gap with peers.

Consumer Acceptability

Consumer acceptability is generally a qualitative measure. Data from stakeholders reveal their perceptions of RTI in relation to curriculum, instruction, management, and leadership. This information is generally garnered through focus groups and surveys which are best conducted by an external facilitator or evaluation consultant. While the primary focus of this evaluation component is teachers and school-level administrators, the primary implementers, district leadership, and parents should not be excluded.

Systems Change

Systems change examines data trends and provides a big-picture view of RTI impact. Potential data sources include special education exit rates, progress of disaggregated groups (for example, gender, racial, or income disparity), improvement between schools and districts, and progress towards measurable objectives. Statewide and nationally normed assessments provide much of the necessary comparison data. Cohort comparisons are particularly valuable when tracing multiyear impact. Cohort comparisons trace the same group of students from one time period to the next rather than comparing dissimilar groups. Comparing third graders at ABC Elementary in 2007 to the same group of fourth graders in 2008 provides statistically more reliable data comparisons than using data from 2007 third graders and comparing them to 2008 third graders. Although mobility factors influence validity, cohorts are generally better measures than year-to-year comparisons of the same grade level. Systems change also incorporates RTI's impact on curriculum alignment, professional development, and redistribution of fiscal and personnel resources.

Implementation Fidelity

Implementation fidelity creates an accountable system, and it is the most complex to evaluate. RTI is a framework, not a program, so there is flexibility between districts and schools. The components remain the same, but the implementation methodology differs. Schools are allowed to implement the key components of RTI, shaping them to fit the school population, root causes, neighborhood characteristics, and resources. However, this also creates a trap, particularly within large districts—that of consistency between schools.

Schools must be held accountable to the same implementation standards. For example, an effective Problem-Solving Team has specific characteristics. They meet regularly, examine student data as part of the problem-solving process, include multisector input like parents, classroom teachers, and experts, and create actionable, time-limited plans for student interventions. Each site must incorporate those specific characteristics and become highly proficient in delivering them. The implementation may be different, but the standard remains the same, just as in classroom instruction. We find that districts establish measurable goals for RTI, provide foundational RTI training, send the trainees back to their schools to create an RTI system, and then wait for the miraculous outcomes. Unfortunately, district leadership hopes to minimize costs by eliminating or minimizing district oversight during RTI implementation. This is the equivalent of standing at the edge of a chasm, telling schools they have to get everyone to the other side, providing pole-vaulting instruction, and then waiting for success. *Success cannot happen without active coaching and progress monitoring of the implementation process.*

Thus, evaluating implementation fidelity requires investigation on two levels. Level 1 investigates the structure of RTI. Level 2 investigates the systemic incorporation of RTI. Both levels must incorporate district and school activities.

Table 8-1 (below) and Table 8-2 (page 125) outline a possible evaluation process.

Table 8-1. Fidelity of Implementation Level 1: RTI Structure

	DISTRICT-LEVEL EXAMPLE	SCHOOL-LEVEL EXAMPLE
LEADERSHIP	• Commitment has been made for 3 years of RTI implementation resources.	• Consensus is built. • Schedules and credits are aligned to accommodate strategic and intensive interventions.

MANAGEMENT	• RTI foundational training is provided to school teams.
	• RTI–SPED policies have been developed.
		• RTI professional development for staff is provided.
		• Problem-Solving Team is in place.
		  - Functionality has been defined, including regular meeting times and resources (substitutes, copying funds, access to electronic data, access to student records, and so on).
		  - Policies and procedures are established, including forms to be used as part of the RTI process, methods of communicating with teachers and parents, and dealing with RTI–SPED issues.

INSTRUCTION	• Research-based interventions at each tier are supported by district specialists. • Research-based interventions at each tier are supported by professional development.	• 1–2 research-based interventions are included at each tier.
CURRICULUM	• Curriculum is aligned across the district.	• The curriculum is effective for core Tier 1 instruction.
ASSESSMENT	• External evaluation structure is in place.	• Data management system for progress monitoring is available to all teachers. • Teachers and staff regularly use data to improve Tier 1 instruction.

Table 8-2. Fidelity of Implementation Level 2:
RTI Systemic Incorporation

	DISTRICT-LEVEL EXAMPLE	SCHOOL-LEVEL EXAMPLE
LEADERSHIP	• Commitment has been made for 3 years of RTI implementation resources.	• The principal provides instructional leadership. • The principal uses classroom observations to monitor instructional fidelity.

MANAGEMENT	• RTI standards are maintained across sites.
	• Coaching and mentoring are provided.
	• Data management is practiced.
		• Problem-Solving Team is in place.
		  - Functionality is high.
		  - Use of data is prevalent.
		  - Parent involvement is high.
		  - Research-based interventions are used.
		• Inservice is provided for school staff.
		• Student Action Plans are created based on data.

INSTRUCTION	• Data are used to differentiate instruction. • Interventions are delivered with fidelity.	• Only research-based interventions are used. • Interventions are delivered with fidelity according to publisher research. For example, Read 180® requires a 90-minute intervention to maximize effectiveness. Instruction for less than 90 minutes decreases the potential for student success. • Student Action Plans are implemented with fidelity. • Effective Tier 1 differentiated instruction is provided.
CURRICULUM	• Tier 1 curriculum is effective with the various populations in district schools. • Tier 2 and 3 curricula are effective with targeted populations.	• Curricula at all tiers are delivered with fidelity.
ASSESSMENT	• Student outcomes • Consumer acceptability • Systems change • Implementation fidelity	• Feedback from the principal and other administrators is used to ensure fidelity of classroom instruction and interventions. • The Problem-Solving Team monitors efficacy of action planning, progress monitoring, and student improvement.

Depending on the size of the district and available resources, it may be preferable to evaluate only Level 1 in year one, and add Level 2 in subsequent years. Districts should differentiate between an evaluation of RTI Problem-Solving Teams and referral structures versus RTI's translation into practice within the classroom.

Graphic Data

As districts create RTI systems, graphic data become powerful representations of change on all levels. The following graphics and figures from Colorado Springs School District 11 provide some examples.

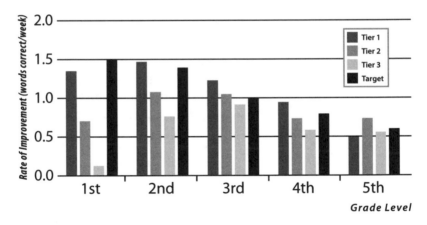

**Figure 8-2. DIBELS Oral Reading Fluency (ORF)
Rate of Improvement, Fall and Spring**

From Carver Elementary School. © 2008, Colorado Springs School District No. 11. Colorado Springs School District No. 11 hereby permits reproduction of this figure for educational use.

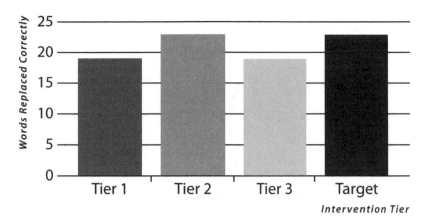

Figure 8-3. Maze Seventh Grade Reading Comprehension (Spring 2007)

From Holmes Middle School. © 2008, Colorado Springs School District No. 11. Colorado Springs School District No. 11 hereby permits reproduction of this figure for educational use.

By quantifying data by tiers, RTI staff, leadership, and stakeholders immediately grasp that students at risk in Tiers 2 and 3 are achieving at rates similar to Tier 1 students.

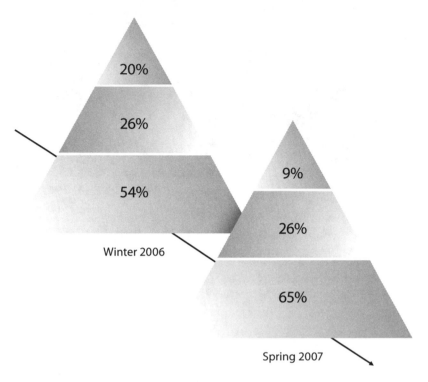

Figure 8-4. Percentage of Students by Tier

*From Hunt Elementary School. © 2008, Colorado Springs School District No. 11.
Colorado Springs School District No. 11 hereby permits reproduction of this
figure for educational use.*

Notice the movement from students out of Tier 3 and into
Tier 1, indicating that RTI is reducing student reading gaps.

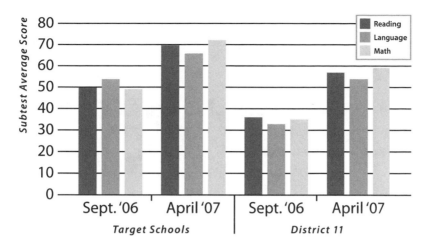

Figure 8-5. Fourth Grade TerraNova Achievement: Target Schools Compared With All Other District Schools

© *2008, Colorado Springs School District No. 11. Colorado Springs School District No. 11 hereby permits reproduction of this figure for educational use.*

Graphs based on standardized assessment data enabled district leadership to illustrate the impact of RTI at its exemplar schools compared with schools not yet implementing RTI or in the beginning stages.

Just as assessment is critical to student improvement, systemic evaluation enables RTI to move forward systemically. Data have the power to point up gaps in current instructional practices and RTI implementation. More importantly, data and its analysis provide the basis for creating the pathway to sustainable excellence, as we shall see in the next chapter.

Chapter 9

Sustainability

RTI sustainability begins before implementation and culminates in the systemic integration of root cause analysis in the areas of team functioning, data management and application, intervention strategies, and parent involvement.

Mike Schmoker's *Results Now: How We Can Achieve Unprecedented Improvements in Teaching and Learning* (2006) lays out the dilemma of educational improvement in the United States. Schmoker's premise, which we accept, is 1) educational improvement suffers from poor leadership at most levels—federal, state, and local, and 2) most initiatives are complicated in design, void of buy-in, chaotic in implementation, and lacking in internal impetus. Leadership is the lynchpin for educational improvement resulting in consistent, high-quality student achievement. Without leadership, sustainability is only a 14-letter word.

RTI can be initiated using few monetary and physical resources. Most of what is required by school districts and schools already exists, but may not be organized effectively or implemented with fidelity. One medium-sized middle school placed on adequate yearly progress watch by the state department of education, due to nonimprovement of student achievement, had an art teacher on staff who happened to be trained in strategic reading. The school also had several special education teachers on staff, members who were serving students in groups based on the students' identified disabilities. In addition, the school had a reading specialist teacher, a counselor with skills in data management, and a social worker committed to behavioral interventions. The staff worked in the traditional isolation model of most school staffs prior to RTI restructuring. Furthermore, several scientifically based intervention programs had been purchased for the school and were in use, but not according to the published requirements of the programs. After RTI restructuring, the staff assumed roles based on their greatest talents and the needs of the new RTI design. Staff members, along with the principal, designed an effective RTI plan for their school.

Improved student scheduling was a priority. The entire school staff redesigned a pyramid of intervention based on student needs, ensured fidelity of treatment through the training of staff members, and allocated adequate time for interventions. The special education staff began teaching general and special education students together in preventative math and reading intervention groups. The art teacher assisted the reading specialist in an arts and reading program. The counselor led the RTI problem-solving process for the school, and the social worker and a team designed a schoolwide behavioral intervention plan and programs. Grade-level teachers took charge of all Tier 1 interventions and collaborated with support staff in Tier 2 interventions. In one year, this school made dramatic improvement in student achievement becoming a school recognized for improvement excellence.

Simultaneously, radical changes were taking place at the central office. The directors of supplemental programs began to meet together for the first time, specifically for districtwide RTI implementation. The directors created a professional learning community dedicated to improved, districtwide student achievement. The director of special education met regularly with the director of the English-Language Learners program, the director of Title I programs, and the director of grants. Targeted, districtwide professional development was designed to support classroom teachers and specialists delivering interventions. A districtwide audit of interventions was utilized to design a districtwide pyramid of intervention at all levels. Budget plans were developed cooperatively so that the money available for professional development and program improvements had a stronger, cross-program impact than budget planning in isolation. In fact, a consolidated budget was designed to increase impact of available resources for all students in need. Through these collaborative models, no additional resources were required to implement RTI; rather, resources were redesigned and redeployed to meet student needs.

Regardless of a district's perceived use of resources, they require 1) a foundation of collegiality in a professional learning community that believes all children *will* learn, 2) a well-aligned, standards-based, rigorous curriculum where educators know what students need to know, 3) a way to determine if students are learning what they need to know, and 4) a plan for what to do when students are not learning (DuFour, DuFour, & Eaker, 2005). It is this last element that defines RTI—rather like the Ogden Nash (1940) poem:

> There was a little chigger
> That wasn't any bigger
> Than the wee small head of a pin.
> But the bump that it raises
> Itches like blazes,
> And that's where the rub comes in.

This defines the dilemma of RTI implementation in a system that is poorly responsive to individual student needs. We have experienced RTI implementation in school systems where the curriculum is not aligned, learning communities have not been taken to scale, assessments are complicated and arranged in a crazy quilt of ill-aligned instruments, and the environment is focused on teaching versus learning. In these systems, RTI raises the weaknesses of the educational environment and puts them on the radar screen for everyone to see—and those bumps do more than "itch like blazes." Consequently, leaders in weak systems should expect resistance until strong leaders from the board of education, the superintendent, and instructional staff can remove the institutional constructs that buffer educators from outside inspection, interference, and disruption of routine habits.

Attempting to build RTI in dysfunctional systems results in systemic low student achievement except for "islands of excellence" formed by principals and teachers who do care and do not resent outside evaluation. Due to the numerous educational systems that continue to perpetrate chaotic change versus strategic student-outcome improvement, it is possible that RTI may fail on a national level in spite of any federal or state mandates. RTI could become one more educational initiative that did not work. Failure may occur in spite of the overwhelming data demonstrating the success of RTI in preventing basic skills deficits, and RTI's ability to positively impact the performance of underachieving students. Nationwide, RTI failure may occur if leadership does not focus on the fidelity of RTI's systemic and systematic implementation and if leadership rejects the obligation to create an accountable and transparent process.

Conducting Root Cause Analysis for RTI Development

Sustainability begins with root cause analysis, prior to RTI implementation.

High-quality root cause analysis is lacking in most new RTI development in districts and schools. This oversight occurs in the absence of an effective continuous quality improvement (CQI) process. The CQI process, when implemented correctly:

- Provides a well-defined system of evaluation using student-based assessments

- Applies measures to monitor what educators are achieving with their students on a daily basis

- Guides staff in evaluating and acting on the results of students' work

CQI closely links what teachers teach, and to what degree students are learning what is taught. Most importantly, it establishes systems to assist educators to evaluate and act on the results of their work. As in scientific experimentation, broad systematic (routinely used) and systemic (built into the everyday work of schools) educational improvement requires the elimination of "extraneous" variables from a controlled environment.

Examples of extraneous variables include:

- Teaching staff who lack the capacity to provide strategic and differentiated reading and math skills instruction

- Weak assessment and data management systems that have low validity and reliability, providing poor data to teachers and administrators

   - Systems for interpreting data that are cumbersome and not user-friendly, challenging to implement, and requiring multiple steps to disaggregate data

   - Systems that do not provide timely formative and summative data to instructional staff, resulting in the inability of data to inform instruction

- Lack of systematic and systemic processes for reviewing formative (frequent, classroom-based) student performance data including Looking at Student Work, an authentic and immediate way to see how students are doing

- Lack of systematic and systemic processes for reviewing summative student performance data (high-stakes testing, nationally normed assessments, or exit exams)

- Poor alignment between curriculum, instruction, formative assessment, and high-stakes testing in a time-relevant and sequential manner to ensure student success

- Lack of pacing guides to assist teachers in establishing course proficiency expectations throughout the school year

- Absence of a school or district professional learning community that emphasizes continual improvement of the *adult* teaching and learning environment

As a district eliminates or minimizes the extraneous variables, it is able to establish its control variables and its independent variable. The control variables are those items that remain the same throughout implementation, such as the district management philosophy and strategic plan, average class size, staffing formulas, and hiring practices. In this situation, we make the assumption that the learner stays constant. He or she is the dependent variable; the changes occur within the selections of the interventions and the frequency, intensity, and duration of delivery. This allows the Problem-Solving Team to determine how well the selected independent variables are working. This process can be used by Problem-Solving Teams for individual students, as well as for leadership teams at the school and district levels. This flexibility is a strength of RTI—the instructional leaders and the teachers adjust based on student needs.

How then does the district test hypotheses or root causes that lead to districtwide improvement? Just as an RTI system establishes goals for individual students with an aim line and a trend line, the District Round Table establishes aim and trend lines for aggregate student groups across the district in each tier of instruction or intervention. The Round Table Team becomes the Problem-Solving Team for districtwide implementation. Root cause analysis and hypothesis testing are second only to leadership in ensuring successful RTI implementation. The following are two examples of this process.

Example #1: Discipline Issues

Sometimes the methods for correcting student behavior become a matter of habit. Little thought is given to the impact on the school's primary role, and to when, where, why, and how students are being disciplined. The following example outlines the root cause analysis experience of a high-poverty elementary school.

Step 1: Conduct Problem Identification

An elementary school led by a dynamic principal accepted the belief that the staff's behavior had a direct impact on the low and flat performance of their students. The result was an achievement gap between where their students performed and where they should be performing. The staff had already implemented the academic component of RTI, but had held off on the behavioral component of the system.

Representative school staff went through a root cause analysis process with two district leaders. They determined that the lack of student behavioral skills in a learning environment was the outstanding variable that was holding back quality teaching and quality learning.

Step 2: Gather Data and Evidence

The staff analyzed school data that had been gathered by the social worker. The data included:

- Type, prevalence, location, and severity rates of referrals from the Positive Behavior Support tracking system
- Types of transition programs effective for students of low income and minority backgrounds with high mobility rates
- Ancillary information on disruptive community issues

The data, once totaled, were startling to the staff. Too much time was spent on discipline, yet discipline did not seem to improve student behavior. Specific targets were established, based on the data collection analysis, and staff underwent training in a schoolwide Positive Behavior Support system.

Step 3: Identify the Key Issue

Commonalities in the data revealed that during the past year, the traditional discipline systems used at all affected grade levels did not appear to have aligned school expectations with the needs, expectations, or resources of minority and low-income students and their families. Students were struggling with the school environment, and appeared to be challenging school rules and acting aggressively toward classmates in group settings. The staff data demonstrated that rules tended to be stated in negative terms such as "Do not run in the halls!" Staff were not highly visible during transitions between classes, and corrective instructions to students were given in negative versus positive terms. Students were recognized for "bad" behavior and not for the behaviors the staff wanted students to develop. Staff members were inconsistent in discipline, and some students were often singled out.

Step 4: Find the Root Cause

Staff accepted the data that revealed a high rate of student off-task behaviors and an inconsistent, unsuccessful, and negative discipline system.

Step 5: Develop Solution Recommendations

School and district leadership identified several preventative systems for students, staff, and parents that are designed to assist the identified student population needs. The District Round Table recommended that schools choose one of the two interventions with the best research outcomes. The Positive Behavior Support program was one of the programs recommended to the school, and was ultimately selected by staff and parents. Goals were established to begin the process of measuring improvement.

Goal: Expulsions will be reduced by 100%, suspensions will be reduced by 75%, and student discipline office and home referrals will be reduced by 75%. Data will be evaluated quarterly to determine if the goal is meeting aim and trend lines as well as to see adjustments that are required.

Step 6: Implement the Solutions

The school leadership implemented a district-recommended program with fidelity. Weekly data were collected on specific student behaviors, and data analysis was conducted weekly to determine if interventions were working.

Step 7: Retest Solutions Based on Data Collection

Adjustments were made to plans, and students were referred to an individual school's Problem-Solving Team if they were not responding to preventative measures.

Step 8: Align Data From Steps 1–7 to Determine Prevention Strategies

At the end of the second quarter, the staff examined the outcome data. Additionally, the team discussed how to improve the discipline process to prevent similar problems in the coming year. Prevention strategies included summer school preparation for students who were new to the city. These programs were designed to quickly assess and remediate learning deficiencies prior to school enrollment, coordinating the academic pyramid with the behavioral component of the pyramid. Students enrolling later were provided quick assessments and tutoring or intervention programs immediately, commensurate with their classes. Policies were changed, and recommendations were made accordingly.

Example #2: Reading Issues

In this example, a principal and a fourth grade PLC examined the reasons behind their students' lack of achievement. Rather than just focusing on what the students did not learn, they focused on the "why"—defining the causes of the teaching and learning failure and how to correct it.

Step 1: Conduct Problem Identification

At another school, 80% of fourth graders did not meet the winter benchmark for midyear assessment in reading.

Step 2: Gather Data and Evidence

Analysis of scores demonstrated common themes of low performance in vocabulary and reading comprehension. Specifically, students could not adequately summarize a paragraph, and their vocabulary skills had not improved from the fall benchmark.

Step 3: Identify the Key Issue

Additional analysis of student performance in reading comprehension for this group demonstrated weaknesses in retell skills.

Step 4: Find the Root Cause

The district staff conferred with elementary literacy, curriculum, and instruction specialists. The group determined that the district curriculum in *third* grade lacked rigor in nonfiction reading and vocabulary development. Furthermore, *fourth*-grade instruction did not stress higher order thinking skills, and teachers were weak in their ability to scaffold literacy concepts into core subjects other than reading.

Step 5: Develop Solution Recommendations

1. Building leadership teams and literacy resource coaches will work with all district fourth grade teachers to provide classroom interventions, including vocabulary development, reading comprehension, and retell and summarization skills.

2. Embedded staff development will be provided to all fourth-grade teachers on literacy resource coaching and professional learning communities.

3. District-level literacy, curriculum, and instruction staff will revise the third-grade reading curriculum to increase rigor.

Step 6: Implement the Solutions

All three solutions will be implemented immediately.

> **G**oal 1: All fourth graders will demonstrate adequate rate of improvement in reading comprehension and vocabulary as demonstrated on curriculum-based measurements and spring benchmarks to meet trend and aim line goals prior to end-of-year testing.
>
> **G**oal 2: Third-grade and, if necessary, fourth-grade curriculums will be revised by the end of the school year.

Step 7: Retest Solutions Based on Data Collection

Classroom data will be collected weekly to determine progress in vocabulary development and comprehension using Maze reading probes. The weekly analysis will be evaluated to determine if the plan is working. If the plan is not working within 4 weeks, more intensive services will be provided to students. Students are expected to demonstrate trajectory for meeting end-of-year goals.

Step 8: Align Data From Steps 1–7 to Determine Prevention Strategies

The District Round Table will continue to monitor fourth-grade reading progress. The curricular changes to third grade plus the embedded staff development are prevention strategies. The Round Table should spend time over the summer aligning high-stakes data to formative outcomes and then monitor fourth-grade assessment data in the fall to gauge the impact of changes to curriculum and instruction.

Failure of districts to set districtwide hypotheses can be observed in low and flat student progress on high-stakes testing in core academic areas. High representation of minority and low-income groups in student discipline referrals with little or no decrease in suspensions, expulsions, or dropouts indicates the failure of districts to use an evidenced-based process to improve student outcomes.

Preventing RTI Failure

Improving student achievement and success requires changing how education does business.

So what *is* needed to sustain RTI for student improvement? *Without a doubt, implementation fidelity and leadership are the two elements that determine RTI success or failure.* We recommend the following checklist to assist leaders in eliminating or reducing the risks of RTI failure.

Ten-Point RTI Sustainability Checklist

1. The board of education participates in RTI professional development and demonstrates a working knowledge of RTI concepts and implementation strategies.

2. The board of education has led town hall meetings to gather input from citizens and staff on RTI, identifying its purpose, essential components, why it is being considered for implementation, and the anticipated results. A consensus-building process has been utilized with the attendees to solidify a common direction.

3. The superintendent and his or her staff have incorporated RTI into the district's student improvement plan. The plan addresses the key components of RTI and specifically commits resources for implementation in literacy, math, and student behavior, at a minimum. All solutions

are aligned to state standards and incorporate accountability measures. All staff are held accountable for RTI implementation *with fidelity*. (A checklist for assessing fidelity is included in appendix C, page 167).

4. An assessment system has been endorsed by the central administration that supports curriculum-based measurement with user-friendly data management. This system is aligned with the district assessments used to measure benchmarks and high-stakes student outcomes. Central administration also supports building-level skill development in data analysis and outcome application.

5. Sufficient professional development supports capacity development for staff and parents to optimize participation in the RTI process.

6. An evaluation plan identifies staff performance indicators delineating when and how RTI fidelity has been achieved in each building, and how it will align with expected student outcomes.

7. A districtwide District Round Table Team exists to assist with the continuous quality improvement of RTI. This team uses input from stakeholders to continue to minimize untoward variables and improve or maintain effective variables. This group establishes the accountability measures for the district.

8. District leadership endorses professional learning communities by continuously supporting the tenants of a PLC environment for teachers and students, and provides the vision of RTI through ongoing two-way quality communication.

9. Student and staff outcomes are honored publicly by leadership and peers.

10. Measures are continually looped back to RTI leadership and then on to the board of education and superinten-

dent so that they can evaluate outcomes, implement change, and support fidelity improvement.

Evaluating RTI Success

It is critical to have preset measures on how to evaluate the success of RTI as a system for student improvement in academics and behavior. We have devised the following formulas.

Tier 1: Universal Instruction

- At least 80–90% of the student population is either performing at or very near proficiency as measured by benchmarks leading to annual high-stakes testing.
- Schools demonstrate significant decreases in student discipline referrals, dropout rates, suspensions, and expulsions.

Tier 2: Targeted Intervention

- About 10–15% of the student population is demonstrating at least 2 years' growth in a year of intervention, or twice the rate of improvement of students in Tier 1 instruction.
- Targeted students demonstrate significant decreases in student discipline referrals, dropout rates, suspensions, and expulsions.

Tier 3: Intensive Intervention

- About 1–5% of the student population is demonstrating at least 1 year's growth for a year of intervention, or at least 50% of the rate of growth of students in Tier 2.

- Targeted students demonstrate significant decreases in student discipline referrals, dropout rates, suspensions, and expulsions.

Unfortunately, as Schmoker (2006) states, changes in leadership at the board, superintendent, central office, or school levels tend to result in changes in direction for the linkage of curriculum, discipline practices, and program materials. This vicious cycle must be stopped when evidence demonstrates strong student improvement is occurring, particularly in closing the gaps between subgroup student achievement. Data should be archived for continuous quality improvement purposes, and new leadership should be hired or trained so that they can actively increase the educational infrastructure's capacity for sustained success. RTI requires a new way of doing business.

RTI, as we have defined it, requires hard work by everyone involved in the education community. It requires strong and brave leadership at all levels of a school district. It is a systemic and systematic process, requiring transparency and openness of all involved in ongoing evaluation, and acting aggressively when students are not learning what is being taught. RTI requires educational reform.

Why bother? Compelling evidence shows that educators can actually close achievement gaps for the most challenged learners in their schools. This is in addition to the abundant research addressed in this book which demonstrates the significant positive impact of early intervention on student achievement, particularly in reading. Arguably, the most compelling reason to implement RTI successfully is the ability of educators to significantly impact the ability of students to become lifelong successful readers, as observed in the pre- and post-intervention brain imaging data referred to in chapter 1. From this work comes the most important reason for RTI to be implemented effectively: For the satisfaction of students, teachers, and administrators when students succeed as never before.

Appendices

Appendix A

Research

The impetus for Response to Intervention was derived from the 1997 amendments to the Individuals with Disabilities Education Act (IDEA), its renewal in 2004, the No Child Left Behind Act (NCLB), and research-based recommendations from the Report of the National Reading Panel (2000), the National Association of State Directors of Special Education, and the National Research Center on Learning Disabilities.

Tiered intervention models were developed in the late 1980s and 1990s and provided baseline data and instructional direction for special education students. Most models incorporate increasing intervention intensity, progress monitoring, instructional adjustment, and an eventual decrease in the array and intensity of interventions, all based on individual student response. The models are now expanding to strategically target general education students with significant learning or behavioral discrepancies.

States, districts, and schools are jumping on the RTI bandwagon. On the plus side, RTI organizes research-based practices into a multifaceted learning system responsive to individual student needs. On the downside, schools and districts experience mixed success.

How, then, does a district or school decide to incorporate RTI? Is it a valid construct? What does the research say? Bottom line, will RTI significantly improve achievement of the lowest performing students and strengthen instruction for all students?

To understand RTI research, the reader must realize that RTI is a framework for optimizing learning. It is not a program to be pulled off the shelf and inserted into the classroom to "fix" academic achievement or performance. RTI changes how instruction and instructional leadership occur in the classroom, school, and district.

Because RTI is not a program, the research must be examined at two levels. First, what pros and cons does the research reveal about the basic components of an RTI model? Second, what does research reveal about systemic implementation? This component is particularly important for districts and schools interested in moving RTI from a special education model to a general education model.

Basic Components of an RTI Model

The National Association of State Directors of Special Education and key researchers developed the following definition for RTI:

RTI is the practice of 1) providing high-quality instruction/intervention matched to student needs and 2) using learning rate over time and level of performance to 3) make important educational decisions. (Batsche, Elliott, Grimes, Kovaleski, Prasse, Reschly, Schrag, & Tilly III, 2005, p. 5)

This definition incorporates the basic components necessary for an effective RTI system: instruction and interventions, formative data, and implementation fidelity.

High-Quality Instruction and Interventions

Teachers

Arguably the most critical component of any educational system is the competency of its teachers. Hanushek (1992) found that students with a very high-quality teacher can gain the equivalent of 1.5 grade levels, while students with a poor-quality teacher will gain only .5 grade levels. Similarly, Sanders and Horn (1994) found a 39 percentage-point differential in high-stakes test achievement between students with the most and least effective teachers. For schools struggling to achieve adequate yearly progress benchmarks, Robert Marzano's meta-analysis should also be noted. Marzano found that "school-level and teacher-level factors account for approximately 20 percent of the variance in student achievement" (Mid-Continent Research for Education and Learning, 2003, p. 3). While this percentage is small compared to student background knowledge, intelligence, and home environment, it is enough to move students in effective classrooms from partially proficient to advanced achievement levels.

Other researchers confirm that teacher quality not only positively impacts student success but is also cumulative (Sanders, 1999; Sanders & Horn, 1994; Waters, Marzano, & McNulty, 2003). In other words, students with high-quality teachers for several years build on achievement, widening the gap with students from classrooms with lower quality instruction. This is of particular concern since there are indications that minority students are assigned more frequently to ineffective teachers than to the highest quality teachers (Sanders & Rivers, 1996).

Instruction

How, then, can a teacher positively impact student academic success and positive behavior? One methodology is differentiated instruction. This topic has existed for decades and has spawned many definitions. Vygotsky's social development theory (1978) proposes that learning is a lifelong developmental process dependent on social interaction. If students are to learn, then teachers must be collaborators in that process.

Learning in safe environments is aligned with much of behavioral and cognitive science. In an operant conditional model, when learning is followed by a positive reinforcer, it is likely to happen again (Skinner, 1953; Omrod, 1999). Social learning theory focuses on modeling and positive feedback (Bandura, 1971). Students observe acceptable learning behavior, model the behavior if they feel safe, and receive positive feedback, which regulates future behavior. Maslow's (1970) hierarchy of needs also conveys the individual's necessity to feel safe and have basic needs met before self-actualization begins. Students who feel uncomfortable or fearful in the classroom learn poorly, if at all. High stress causes the brain to move its ability to create and organize thought from the cortex to the limbic system, where physical reaction is the problem solver. In *Teaching with the Brain in Mind*, Eric Jensen explains that "the systems [for thinking and feeling] are so interconnected that chemicals of emotion are released virtually simultaneously with cognition" (1998, p. 93). Strong negative emotions may develop when work is perceived as too difficult, when the student feels unable to respond to the instruction, or personal needs (physical or emotional) displace the need or desire to learn. The latter is particularly prevalent in children of poverty (Payne, 2003).

Once the student feels safe, learning must present a reasonable challenge. What constitutes a challenge depends on the age and development of the learner (Csikszentmihalyi, 1990). Moneta and Csikszentmihalyi (1996) found that when a student is "in the flow," he or she perceives that the task is possible, concentration is maximized, and the student is able to hone skills and abilities to achieve beyond current mastery. Challenging instruction engages the learner so that he or she acquires more independence and self-direction (Hunt, 1961, in Whalen, 2005). Some of the most intriguing research comes from the field of metacognition and the processes of problem-solving. By introducing curriculum and instructional methods that are just beyond the student's current abilities, metacognition focuses learning on recognizing new material, deciding how to tackle the difficult subject, where to start, how to deconstruct the project, how to access expert advice, and how to work towards subject mastery (Conner, 2002).

Finally, instruction must be contextual to the student's prior experience (Greeno, 1997; Lave & Wenger, 1991). As a process, learning involves active organization and synthesis of the skills, facts, and concepts being presented (Corley, 2005). This includes accessing prior knowledge and vocabulary plus incorporating self-direction, investigation, and exploration (Schunk, 2000). Bransford, Brown, and Cocking (2000, p. 27) said, "Students come to the classroom with preconceptions about how the world works. If their initial understanding is not engaged, they may fail to grasp the new concepts and information that are taught, or they may learn them for purposes of a test but revert to their preconceptions outside the classroom." This is true whether the student has previously experienced the exact situation, or content seems less relevant than his or her ability to relate the new learning to previous experience (Anderson, Greeno, Reder, & Simon, 2000; Brown & Kane, 1988; Greeno, 1997).

Learning Problem Identification and Formative Assessment Data

Learning Problem Identification

Identifying learning difficulties opens a can of worms. Beginning in the 1960s in the United States, students with significant learning disabilities could qualify for special education services. Enter I.Q. testing and the discrepancy formula. Students unsuccessful in school were provided services beyond the regular classroom, given that their I.Q. was sufficiently discrepant from federal guidelines. Student needs were identified through testing, parent inputs, and educational specialists after they had failed.

As the years progressed, educators realized two things. First, many special education students were not making adequate progress, condemning them to a permanent special education label. Second, students with obvious learning disabilities were also not making progress, and there were no additional resources to identify and remediate their problems (Reschly, 2003). Revisions in IDEA and NCLB legislation propelled changes in identifying learning difficulties. However, professionals remain challenged as to how to define *learning disabilities* (Epps, Ysseldyke, & McGue, 1984).

Over the past decade, a growing body of research has demonstrated that a dual discrepancy approach may result in the most accurate identification of learning disabilities (Ahern, 2003). The dual discrepancy theory states that a child's learning disability is gauged on a comparison between achievement level and learning rate as compared to peers (Fuchs, Fuchs, & Compton, 2003). This research found that students identified and given remediation using a dual discrepancy system were more successful than those identified through performance-level-only and growth-rate-only approaches.

Using a dual discrepancy formula requires school systems to acknowledge the needs of students who are unsuccessful in school but have traditionally been ineligible for special services. In particular, students with dyslexia have drawn national attention. Reading research combined with magnetic source imaging (MSI) has produced exciting insights on how brain functioning may impact or cause poor reading achievement. Research results demonstrate that the "vast majority of children with serious reading problems show, during engagement in reading tasks, a distinct brain activation profile that is uncommon among children who have never experienced reading difficulties" (Simos, Fletcher, Bergman, Breier, Foorman, Castillo, Davis, Fitzgerald, & Papanicolaou, 2002, p. 1139). Specifically, poor readers or students who lack skills in processing written words typically have greater electrical activity in the right brain hemispheres. This is compared to good readers who exhibit left brain activity, where "the neurophysiological activity in left temporoparietal regions as revealed by MSI reflects the engagement of brain operations that are indispensable components of the brain mechanisms for reading. If these operations are not engaged properly, . . . reading performance and the capacity to acquire reading skills are [sic] severely compromised" (Papanicolaou et al., 2003, p. 608). However, these researchers have also discovered that when the *correct* intervention occurs, "neural systems are altered" and students learn to read (Papanicolaou et al., 2003, p. 610).

Progress Monitoring

Problem identification implies a comparison to some type of benchmark. Teachers use research-based instructional strategies to move student achievement to the benchmark or beyond. Documenting this change is critical to the academic improvement process and predicates the need for multiple assessments and tracking. Since "Teaching Children to Read," the report of the National Reading Panel (National Institute of Child Health and Human Development, 2000), heavy emphasis has been placed on the five components of reading (phonemic awareness, phonics, vocabulary, fluency, and comprehension), benchmarking, and progress monitoring assessments. The University of Oregon's Dynamic Indicators of Basic Early Literacy Skills (DIBELS) is an example of a curriculum-based measurement tool that provides teachers with immediate feedback on student reading skills.

Curriculum-based measurements (CBMs) "are any set of measurement procedures that use direct observation and recording of a student's performance in a local curriculum as a basis for gathering information to make instructional decisions" (Deno, 1987 in Shinn, 1989, p. 62). CBMs measure mastery on a set of skills relevant to a classroom curriculum and, if nationally validated and standardized, provide a score "that is 1) an indicator of competence . . . and 2) a skills profile that describes strengths and weaknesses on the various skills assessed" (Fuchs & Fuchs, 2003) (numbering added). Reliability between observers, test versions, and test occurrences has established curriculum-based measurement as a viable methodology for identifying specific student needs. Extensive research indicates that CBMs are more sensitive to student growth than commercial achievement tests, curriculum-based tests, and teacher-prepared assessments (Marston, Fuchs, & Deno, 1986).

Educational research using control groups was conducted in the early 1980s. Benjamin Bloom compared students who were given formative assessments to evaluate learning to students given assessments as a basis for learning. These students received feedback on their progress, and the teachers used assessment outcomes to modify curriculum and instruction. At the end of the experiment, Bloom (1984) found that the "average student in the Mastery Learning (experimental) group outperformed 85% of the students in the Conventional Learning (control) group—an Effect size of 1.0" (Bloom's results reported in Local Accountability Professional Development Series, 2004).

Paul Black and Dylan Wiliam conducted an exhaustive literature review of the impact of assessments on student achievement (1998). The review shows that formative assessments are particularly effective when teachers work with students to set goals and interventions based on outcomes. Effect sizes ranged from .4 to .7, with greater effects seen for low-achieving students. Thus, the use of formative assessments can be effective in reducing achievement gaps between subgroups. Black and Wiliam emphasized that three conditions must be met in order for the assessment feedback loop to be effective. Teachers must regularly differentiate instruction based on assessment outcomes. Students must also use the outcomes to understand their own learning gaps. Finally, the assessments must include relevant, deep concepts that meaningfully address curriculum content and concept synthesis (1998).

Fuchs, Fuchs, and Hamlett (1989a) assessed changes in instructional efficacy between teachers who used graphed data versus those who did not. Teachers who use plotted goal and trend lines and then revised them as student learning outstripped anticipated goals succeeded in raising student achievement. The effect on standardized achievement tests was the equivalent of .5 standard deviations.

Implementation Fidelity

The third component of RTI is fidelity of its implementation. RTI matches demonstrated student need to educational and behavioral interventions. The greater the need or learning disability, the greater the intervention frequency, intensity, or duration. Tiered interventions have roots in psychological treatment. Interventions in a hierarchy are "unified by response class . . . and ordered in a planned sequence to resolve a problem situation" (Barnett, 2004, p. 66). Behavioral modification theory acknowledges the need for increased resources for children who are resistant to change (Gresham, 1991). Increasing and decreasing intensity is a common parametric design for studying multi-component interventions (Northrup & Gully, 2001; Van Houten & Hall, 2001).

Research indicates that the tiered intervention approach is aligned with the use of formative assessments and the premise of data-based problem-solving coupled with flexible service delivery (Tilly III, Reschly, & Grimes, 1999; Barnett, 2004). Moreover, the initial multi-tiered models, such as Heartland, Iowa Area Education Agency's four-tiered model, grew out of problem-solving structures that apply more resources as the problem intensity increases (Tilly, 2003). In this model, four tiers worked when responding to small numbers of children. However, larger groups were more easily serviced through three tiers. Two tiers create the current schism between special education and regular education services; the two tiers establish a *have and have not* scenario. Children who are proficient in general education are in Tier 1. Those who lack proficiency are said to have a learning disability and are in need of special education, so they are assigned to Tier 2. Tier 2 includes a broad spectrum of children ranging from those who are below grade level but just need additional practice, to those high–needs students requiring one-on-one support.

Data-Driven Instructional Decisions and Professional Learning Communities

Continuous quality improvement evolved from W. Edwards Deming's work in Japan in the 1940s. In CQI, data are used to assess areas of strength and weakness, providing opportunities to gain expertise by honing processes and learning from others. Education has embraced this concept, although it is used more effectively at some schools than others. Key elements include purposeful data collection, effective data management systems, and meaningful discussions that relate data looking inward to individual student and classroom needs and data looking outward to programmatic and instructional trends (Mid-Continent Research for Education and Learning, 2003).

In one study, Fuchs and Fuchs (2003, p. 2) concluded that teachers who used formative data to guide instruction "generated instruction plans that were statistically significantly more varied and more responsive to individuals' learning needs." More importantly, student achievement was greater than those who lacked time-sensitive data on students' strengths and challenges with effect sizes ranging from .65 to 1.23 standard deviations (Fuchs, Fuchs, & Hamlett, 1989b; Fuchs, Fuchs, Hamlett, & Allinder, 1991; Fuchs, Fuchs, Hamlett, & Stecker, 1990).

However, "data have the capacity to reveal strength and weakness, failure and success" (Schmoker, 1996, p. 33). Data can challenge current practice and upset established routines, and almost always point to some kind of action that should be taken (National Education Association Teaching and Learning Team, 2000). Data can be uncomfortable, particularly without a structure for honest, supportive, collegial discussion. Enter professional learning communities.

Professional learning communities (PLCs) are supportive, interactive groups of teachers and administrators who come together to improve the quality of student learning. Key components of successful PLCs are the willingness to accept constructive feedback while working towards personal, departmental or grade level, and schoolwide improvement (Louis & Kruse, 1995). In Richard DuFour's (2003) words, professional learning communities "use collaboration as a catalyst to change their practices." Other outcomes for PLCs cited in research include decreased teacher isolation, improved classroom practices, professional renewal, and commitment to a continuous quality improvement model (Hord, 1997). Eastwood and Louis (1992) reported that effective PLCs were the most critical element for successful school reform.

Systems Change

Adopting RTI, whether at the building or district level, will change the educational system. A meta-analysis of 30 years of research involving nearly 3,000 schools revealed a correlation of .25 (Waters, Marzano, & McNulty, 2003). In other words, if student achievement and school leadership were rated the same at two schools, and the leadership in school A improves by one standard deviation (as measured on 21 key responsibilities), that change will improve student achievement by 10 percentile points (Waters, Marzano, & McNulty, 2003).

Perhaps the most critical element to RTI success is instructional leadership from the principal, superintendent, and administrative staff. Key findings on education reform from a study by Snipes, Dolittle, & Herlihy (2002) confirmed through meta-analysis by MacIver and Farley (2003) delineated the following steps for RTI success:

1. Create preconditions for reform, including a shared vision and committed resources.

2. Create accountability systems for the process and the outcome.

3. Use central office staff to adopt districtwide curricula and instructional strategies and to provide guidance and support at the building level.

Vision is critical for long-term success (Mahoney, 1990). Through it, the superintendent or principal can hold the system on course through upheaval and uncertainty.

Appendix B

Logic Model

Response to Intervention Logic Model

EXISTING CONDITIONS

Student Needs
- Academic skills • Academic performance • Positive behavior

System Needs
- Academic achievement • Responsive instruction
- Safe, civil learning environment

Parental Needs
- Student academic success • Supportive learning environment

FRAMEWORK FOR CHANGE

Legislative and District Mandates
- NCLB & AYP • IDEA alignment • District achievement plan

RTI Purpose and District Vision
- Improve student achievement and behavior that closes achievement gaps for all students and subgroups.
- By 2014, all students will meet AYP.

Philosophical Framework
- All children can learn. • Early intervention works.
- Removing program silos increases the intervention efficiency and effectiveness.
- Interventions must be structured.

PROCESSES AND INPUTS

Common Direction
- Systemwide articulation of RTI, CQI, PLCs, IEPs, and ILPs
- District RTI Round Table

Instruction
- Discrepancy formula dropped
- District approved list of research-based interventions
- High-quality differentiated instruction
- Professional development in interventions, instructional strategies, formative assessments, and using data to drive instruction

Support Services
- RTI coaches
- Professional development for district and building-level staff

Understanding Response to Intervention
© 2008, Howell, Patton, and Deiotte • www.solution-tree.com

Response to Intervention Logic Model

PROCESSES AND INPUTS CONT'D

Data

- Computer-based student data systems aligned
- Formative and summative assessments correlated
- Regular, frequent data analysis and CQI process

School-Based Systems

- Principal leadership • PST in each building
- RTI implementation that incorporates active student progress monitoring and interventions plus development of policies and procedures
- PLCs and CQI process

MEASUREMENT

Measurement Process

- District goals and objectives • Student goals and objectives
- Consumer satisfaction • Implementation fidelity

Measurement Tools

- CBM or formative assessment data • High-stakes test data
- Behavioral data • Fidelity implementation matrix
- Case studies • Staff development logs
- Teacher, parent, student, and principal surveys and focus groups

DELIVERABLES

Outputs

- Number of staff trained • Number of students in each tier
- Number of schools with PSTs

Outcomes

- Rates of student improvement
- Percentage of students at proficient or advanced levels
- Percentage of students achieving AYP compared to the previous year
- Increased exit rates from special education
- Improved subgroup achievement levels
- Decreased disparity between subgroups

Cost/Benefit and Efficiency Indicators

- Increased instructional time per student
- Decreased disciplinary program costs

Appendix C

Forms

The following forms may assist your district or school with RTI implementation. You may adapt them to your unique needs.

Form 1: RTI Implementation Fidelity Checklist

This checklist is a valuable thermometer for RTI Leadership Teams, Problem-Solving Teams, and coaches to assess your school's progress during the first 3 years of RTI implementation.

- The RTI School Leadership Team should complete Section 1.

- The RTI Problem-Solving Team should complete Section 2.

- The RTI District Leadership Team should complete Section 3.

Forms 2a–c: Problem-Solving Team Intervention Process

These forms are part of the PST and student records and document the student intervention process.

- **Form 2a, Initial Student Referral Form:** This form provides referral and Tier 1 intervention information prior to a PST.
- **Form 2b, Root Cause Analysis Form:** This form prompts the middle steps in the intervention process.
- **Form 2c, Student Action Plan:** This form documents the recommendations from the PST and enables a graphic representation of progress monitoring data.

Form 3: Student Interview Form

This form can be used to gather information from a student prior to a PST.

Forms 4–5: Parent-School Partnership Meeting Invitation and Parent Survey

These forms can be used to invite parents to meet and to gather parent input prior to a PST.

Form 1: RTI Implementation Fidelity Checklist

Section 1: RTI School Leadership Team
Team Basics

		Not Evident	Emerging	Progressing	In Place
1	The school has established an RTI Leadership Team that includes the principal, classroom teachers, and specialists.	☐	☐	☐	☐
2	The RTI Leadership Team has at least one parent representative.	☐	☐	☐	☐
3	RTI research and basic concepts have been presented to all staff members.	☐	☐	☐	☐
4	The RTI Leadership Team is building or has built consensus for adopting RTI as the building's instructional framework.	☐	☐	☐	☐
5	The RTI Leadership Team regularly collaborates with district administration to develop implementation supports.	☐	☐	☐	☐
6	The RTI Leadership Team has developed a pyramid of intervention for the school.	☐	☐	☐	☐
7	The RTI Leadership Team has created a Problem-Solving Team structure that enables parents, classroom teachers, and specialists to participate.	☐	☐	☐	☐

continued on next page →

Form 1 Continued

Section 2: Problem-Solving Team
Team Basics

		Not Evident	Emerging	Progressing	In Place
8	An RTI Problem-Solving Team exists in the building.	☐	☐	☐	☐
9	The team meets regularly.	☐	☐	☐	☐
10	The team has clear procedures for responding promptly to teachers and parents.	☐	☐	☐	☐
11	The team consists of a diverse group of professionals (such as classroom teachers, literacy specialists, counselors, administrators, special education teachers, and so on).	☐	☐	☐	☐
12	The team has an effective method that allows all team members to review relevant data and information prior to the initial RTI Problem-Solving Team meeting on a student.	☐	☐	☐	☐
13	The RTI Problem-Solving Team concentrates on solutions for the student, rather than referral to special education.	☐	☐	☐	☐
14	There are written decision guidelines that are agreed upon for determining tiers of intervention for students.	☐	☐	☐	☐
15	There is effective facilitation and leadership at each team meeting.	☐	☐	☐	☐

Root Cause Analysis

		Not Evident	Emerging	Progressing	In Place
16	Members of the team demonstrate the use of steps in a problem-solving process.	☐	☐	☐	☐
17	Team members demonstrate knowledge of the criteria used for considering a practice or intervention to be research-based.	☐	☐	☐	☐
18	Team members use a reference list of research-based interventions.	☐	☐	☐	☐
19	The team uses data to identify and prioritize student needs and gaps.	☐	☐	☐	☐

Understanding Response to Intervention

168   © 2008, Colorado Springs School District No. 11 • www.solution-tree.com

Colorado Springs School District No. 11 hereby permits reproduction of this form for educational use.

Form 1 Continued

Theory to Practice

		Not Evident	Emerging	Progressing	In Place
20	Teachers receive in-classroom modeling and coaching to support changes in instructional practices.	☐	☐	☐	☐
21	Teachers have developed automaticity in using an array of research-based instructional strategies.	☐	☐	☐	☐
22	Teachers work together in teams and grade level planning to modify and alter instruction for students based on data.	☐	☐	☐	☐

Use of Data

		Not Evident	Emerging	Progressing	In Place
23	The team uses data for various decisions, such as screening, action planning, movement between tiers, progress monitoring, and changes in instruction or interventions.	☐	☐	☐	☐
24	The team has data available at the RTI problem-solving meetings.	☐	☐	☐	☐
25	The team analyzes data using a specific process.	☐	☐	☐	☐
26	The team graphs and charts data.	☐	☐	☐	☐
27	There are agreed-upon written criteria to determine if progress is being made.	☐	☐	☐	☐

Parent Involvement

		Not Evident	Emerging	Progressing	In Place
28	Parents are included in the RTI Problem-Solving Team from the first evidence of concern.	☐	☐	☐	☐
29	Parents are encouraged by team members to be active participants in team meetings and the problem-solving process.	☐	☐	☐	☐
30	Parents are provided with a copy of the RTI intervention plan for their student.	☐	☐	☐	☐
31	Parents receive regular feedback on student progress.	☐	☐	☐	☐

continued on next page →

Form 1 Continued

Section 3: RTI District Leadership Team: Systems Change

Team Basics

	Not Evident	Emerging	Progressing	In Place
32 The team has established an RTI strategic implementation plan.	☐	☐	☐	☐
33 The team meets regularly to discuss RTI implementation.	☐	☐	☐	☐
34 The team uses root cause analysis to identify systemic issues and create systemic solutions.	☐	☐	☐	☐
35 The data collection systems are efficient and useable by all schools.	☐	☐	☐	☐
36 Parent, staff, and administrative feedback is requested to help improve RTI functioning at all levels.	☐	☐	☐	☐

Form 2a: Initial Student Referral Form

Directions: 1) Identify child. 2) Define concern in measurable terms (one concern per page). 3) State the research-based intervention you have implemented for children in your classroom to address this concern (Tier 1, universal intervention.) For each intervention, set up your own measurement specific for this student and record his or her responses. (Informal meetings with the RTI Problem-Solving Team or professional learning community members can help you construct classroom-embedded interventions.) 4) Record any notes from your contacts with parents or conferencing with students. 5) Once classroom measurements are collected, contact the PST.

Student's Name: _____ **Grade/Teacher:** ____ / _____ **Student's Birthday:** __/__/__

Date of Request: __/__/__ **General Concern:** ☐ Behavioral Issue ☐ Academic Issue

Description of Measurable Concern (1 per page)	Classroom Intervention(s)					Measurable Response to Classroom Interventions
	INTERVENTION	FREQUENCY	INTENSITY	DURATION		

Parent Contact Notes:

Student Conference Notes:

Meeting Date and Time:	PST Members:

Form 2b: Root Cause Analysis Form

Additional data and evidence about the problem:

_____

_____

_____

_____

_____

_____

Other issues that contribute to the problem:

_____

_____

_____

_____

_____

_____

Possible root causes (Ask the WHY?):

_____

_____

_____

_____

_____

_____

What are the solution recommendations for the primary causes?

_____

_____

_____

_____

_____

_____

Form 2c: Student Action Plan

Student Name: _____ Grade/Teacher: ___ / _____

Directions: 1) The Problem-Solving Team will create a plan to help achieve the measurable goal. 2) Progress monitoring data will be collected by the assigned person at the determined intervals. 3) A follow-up meeting will be scheduled if intervention results do not reflect targeted growth.

Area of Concern: _____

Measurable Goal: _____

Action Plan: Tentative Date for Follow-Up PST: _____

> What intervention will be used? _____
>
> What is the frequency, intensity, and duration? _____
>
> _____
>
> _____
>
> How often will progress monitoring data be collected? _____
>
> With what instrument? _____
>
> Who will collect the data? _____

Progress Monitoring Data:

Performance Indicator — What will be measured to show that the intervention is effective?															
PM Dates															

Other Comments: _____

_____

_____

_____

Form 3: Student Interview Form

Student Name: _____ Grade: _____

Age: _____ Birthday: _____ Date: _____

Interviewer's Name: _____ Position: _____

Instructions: The interviewer should modify the language in this form to consider the age of the student. *This does not need to be read word-for-word.*

1. What are your greatest strengths? In what areas do you do best? What are you most proud of doing?

   _____

   _____

   _____

2. In what area(s) could you use the most improvement? What things are most difficult for you to do at school?

   _____

   _____

   _____

3. What class gave you the most difficulty last year? What is the one thing you can identify that made it difficult?

   _____

   _____

   _____

4. If we only picked one thing to focus on, what would you like for us to work on that would help you to improve at school?

   _____

   _____

   _____

5. Are you involved in any sports or clubs at school or outside of school? Any organizations?

   _____

   _____

   _____

Understanding Response to Intervention

174   © 2008, Colorado Springs School District No. 11 • www.solution-tree.com

Colorado Springs School District No. 11 hereby permits reproduction of this form for educational use.

6. When you think about the areas you need help improving, think about what helps you learn best.

Curriculum: Are there certain materials, papers, or assignments that make learning more or less difficult (for example, "True/false tests are confusing")? What is your favorite kind of assignment? What is your least favorite kind of assignment?

_____

_____

_____

Instruction: What things does your teacher do that make things more or less difficult (for example, "Directions are sometimes confusing; if I have an advanced organizer for notes, I can follow her lecture better")? What does your favorite teacher do that makes learning easier? What does your least favorite teacher do that makes it hard?

_____

_____

_____

Environment: Are there things about the classroom, or where you study at home, that make learning more or less difficult (for example, "Kids near me want to talk, so I join in")?

_____

_____

_____

Learning: What things do you know about yourself that may offer clues to help us help you be more successful (for example, "If I have to write down assignments, I seem to remember homework better")?

_____

_____

_____

7. If the plan we develop works, how will things be different for you at school?

_____

_____

_____

8. Would you like to be at the meeting to represent yourself and participate in developing a plan, or would you like to have someone represent you and meet with you after the meeting?

_____

_____

_____

Form 4: Parent-School Partnership Meeting Invitation

Dear _____,

As a follow-up to our previous conversation, we would like to invite you to a meeting on ____/____/____ at _____ in _____. The purpose of this meeting is to share information about _____ and to discuss how we can work collaboratively with you to provide school support. Staff members who work with your child will be at the meeting. If there is anyone you would specifically like to attend from school or elsewhere, please let us know. If this time will not work for you, we will reschedule, or we will work with you to find a time to share information.

Attached is a parent survey. This information can help the school staff in learning more about how you see your child. _____ will be contacting you before the meeting to review this survey with you and answer any questions you may have about this process.

Sincerely,

Name
Position
Phone
Email

Form 5: Parent Survey

Student Name: _____ Grade: _____

Teacher:_____ Date:_____

Directions: Please look over the following categories. We are interested in what you think your child's strengths and difficulties are. Identify items you believe are strengths with an "S." Identify items you believe are difficulties with a "D." You can make additional comments on the back of the form.

Reading

_____ Sight words

_____ Word attack skills

_____ Comprehension

_____ Fluency

_____ Pleasure reading

Oral Language

_____ Articulation

_____ Speech fluency

_____ Grammar

_____ Organization of ideas

Work Habits

_____ Attention span

_____ Following directions

_____ Listening skills

_____ Assignment completion

_____ Organization of materials

_____ Time management

_____ Homework

Math

_____ Facts

_____ Understanding of concepts

_____ Understanding of processes

_____ Problem-solving

Written Language

_____ Spelling

_____ Punctuation

_____ Capitalization

_____ Grammar

_____ Handwriting

_____ Sentence structure

_____ Paragraph structure

_____ Ideas about the topic; remaining on topic

Social or Emotional

_____ Happiness

_____ Self-image

_____ Response to stress

_____ Empathy towards others

_____ Peer interactions

_____ Helpfulness to others

_____ Adult interactions

_____ Leadership

_____ Compliance to rules and procedures

_____ Withdrawal

_____ Independence

_____ Physical outbursts

_____ Self-advocacy

_____ Impulsivity

_____ Responsibility

_____ Being a loner

_____ Conflict resolution skills

Appendix D

Frequently Asked Questions

What does "Response to Intervention" mean?

Response to Intervention means students are closely monitored for academic and behavioral progress. The curriculum is modified in the event that an individual student or groups of students are not successful. The continued collection and analysis of data measure how well students are responding to the interventions provided by the teacher or another professional.

Is Response to Intervention only for special education students?

No. Response to Intervention is for any student who is not succeeding in the classroom. This may mean the student is learning at a slower rate or lower level than his or her classmates, or the student is performing significantly below potential.

What is a Problem-Solving Team?

A Problem-Solving Team is made up of a group of teachers and school staff who meet regularly to help design interventions for and monitor progress of students at risk for failure. Different staff members may be part of the team depending on the needs of the student. Parents or guardians are also encouraged to join the team to create an effective action plan for their child.

How do I know my student is progressing?

Response to Intervention uses short, frequent tests (about 1–3 minutes each) to find out if a student is making progress. The results are often displayed using a graph. The graph provides valuable information about student progress and how he or she is performing in relation to a standard benchmark.

Is behavior part of RTI?

Yes. Many students have the knowledge and skills to be successful. However, their behavior may negatively impact their academic success. Schools and classrooms have developed levels of interventions to help students monitor and improve their behavior.

How does negative behavior impact academic achievement?

When a child misbehaves in class, he or she is less likely to be prepared to receive the instruction necessary for academic success. He or she may be distracted or distract others, or miss valuable information, directions, or expectations.

What is the difference between academic skills and academic performance?

Academic skills are those tasks, concepts, and ideas that are grade-level expectations for all students. Academic performance is the student's ability to demonstrate skills by attending class, completing accurate work, taking tests, and staying on task in the classroom.

References and Resources

Ahern, E. (2003, December). Specific learning disability: Current approaches to identification and proposals for change. *Project Forum*. Alexandria, VA: National Association of State Directors of Special Education.

Aldine Independent School District. (2007). *Great schools: The parent guide to K-12 success.* Accessed at www.greatschools.net/cgi-bin/tx/district_profile/83/#students on March 15, 2008.

American Association of School Administrators. (2002). *All means all—Part 2.* Accessed at www.aasa.org/files/PDFs/Publications/Strategies/Strategies_10-02.pdf on September 11, 2005.

American Heritage Dictionary of the English language (4th ed.). (2000). New York: Houghton Mifflin.

Anderson, J., Greeno, J., Reder, L., & Simon, H. (2000). Perspectives on learning, thinking, and activity. *Educational Researcher, 29*(4), 11–13.

Bandura, A. (1971). *Social learning theory.* New York: General Learning Press.

Barnett, D. (2004, July). Response to intervention: Empirically based special service decisions from single-case designs of increasing and decreasing intensity. *Journal of Special Education, 38*(2), 66–79.

Batsche, G., Elliott, J., Grimes, J., Kovaleski, J., Prasse, D., Reschly, D., Schrag, J., & Tilly III, W. (2005). *Response to intervention: Policy considerations and implementation.* Alexandria, VA: National Association of State Directors of Special Education.

Bender, W., & Shores, C. (2007). *Response to intervention: A practical guide for every teacher.* Thousand Oaks, CA: Corwin Press.

Bergan, J., & Kratochwill, T. (1990). *Behavioral consultation and therapy.* New York: Plenum.

Black, P., & Wiliam, D. (1998). Inside the black box: Raising standards through classroom assessment. *Phi Delta Kappan, 80*(2), 139–149.

Bloom, B. (1984). The 2 sigma problem: The search for methods of group instruction as effective as one-on-one tutoring. *Educational Researcher, 13*, 4–16.

Blythe, T., Allen, D., & Powell, B. S. (1999). *Looking together at student work: A companion guide to assessing student learning.* New York: Teachers College Press.

Borman, G., & Rachuba, L. (2001). *Academic success among poor and minority students: An analysis of competing models of school effects (Report #52).* Baltimore: Johns Hopkins University, Center for Research on the Education of Students Placed at Risk. Accessed at www.csos.jhu.edu/crespar/techReports/Report52.pdf on March 1, 2008.

Bottoms, G. (2003). What school principals need to know about curriculum and instruction. *ERS Spectrum, 21*(1), 29.

Bransford, J., Brown, A., & Cocking, R. (Eds.). (2000). How people learn: Brain, mind, experience, and school committee on developments in the science of learning. *Commission on Behavioral and Social Sciences and Education of the National Research Council.* Washington, D.C.: National Academies Press.

Brown, W. (2007). *RtI at Hunt Elementary School.* PowerPoint presented at Colorado Springs School District 11, Colorado Springs, CO.

Brown, A., & Kane, M. (1988). Preschool children can learn to transfer: Learning to learn and learning from example. *Cognitive Psychology, 20*(4), 493–523.

Bruner, J. (1966). *Toward a theory of instruction.* Cambridge, MA: The Belknap Press of Harvard University Press.

California Department of Education. (2008). *Cooperative learning: Elements of successful cooperative learning.* Accessed at www.cde.ca.gov/sp/el/er/cooplrng.asp on March 9, 2008.

Carter, G. (2004). *A call to close the gap.* Accessed at www.ascd.org/portal/site/ascd/menuitem.ef397d712ea0a4a0a89ad324d3108a0c/template.article?articleMgmtId=9c920f05c1520010VgnVCM1000003d01a8c0RCRD on September 12, 2005.

Csikszentmihalyi, M. (1990). *Flow: The psychology of optimal experience.* New York: HarperCollins.

Colorado Department of Education. (2006, Fall). *Pupil mem-bership.* Accessed at www.cde.state.co.us/cdereval/rv2006pmlinks.htm on February 3, 2008.

Colorado Springs School District 11. (2006). *Response to intervention website information.* Accessed at www.d11.org/rti on February 3, 2008.

Conner, M. L. (2002). *A primer on educational psychology.* Accessed at www.agelesslearner.com/intros/edpsych.html on February 3, 2008.

Corley, M. (2005, March). *Differentiated instruction: Adjusting to the needs of all learners.* Boston, MA: National Center for the Study of Adult Learning and Literacy. Accessed at www.ncsall.net/?id=736 on February 3, 2008.

Crowell, R., & Tissot, P. (1986). *Curriculum alignment.* Elmhurst, IL: North Central Regional Educational Laboratory.

Dauber, S., & Epstein, J. (1991). School programs and teacher practices of parent involvement in inner-city elementary and middle schools. *Elementary School Journal, 91,* 289–306.

Deno, S. (1987). Curriculum-based measurement. *Teaching Exceptional Children, 20*(1), 41–47.

Deno, S., Espin, C., & Fuchs, L. (2002). Evaluation strategies for preventing and remediating basic skill deficits. In M. R. Shinn, H. M. Walker, & G. Stoner (Eds.), *Interventions for achievement and behavior problems II: Preventive and remedial approaches* (pp. 213–242). Bethesda, MD: National Association of School Psychologists.

Derlet, R. (2004). Triage. *eMedicine.* Accessed at www.emedicine. com/emerg/topic670.htm on July 5, 2007.

DuFour, R. (2003). Leading edge: "Collaboration lite" puts student achievement on a starvation diet. *Journal of Staff Development, 24*(3).

DuFour, R., DuFour, R., & Eaker, R. (Eds.). (2005). *On common ground: The power of professional learning communities.* Bloomington, IN: Solution Tree (formerly National Educational Service).

Eastwood, K., & Louis, K. (1992). Restructuring that lasts: Managing the performance dip. *Journal of School Leadership, 2*(2), 213–224.

Education Trust. (2004). *Latino achievement in America.* Accessed at www2.edtrust.org/NR/rdonlyres/7DC36C7E-EBBE-43BB-8392-CDC618E1F762/0/ LatAchievEnglish.pdf on September 12, 2005.

Education Trust. (2007). *ESEA: Myths versus reality—Answers to common questions about the new No Child Left Behind Act.* Accessed at www2.edtrust.org/EdTrust/Template%20 Files/esea.aspx?NRMODE=Published&NRO RIGINALURL=%2fEdTrust%2fESEA%2fESEA%2bG eneral%2ehtm&NRNODEGUID=%7b688130FF-C97A-46F3-A4C7-4EB518F80173%7d&NRCACHEHINT=G uest#myth on March 30, 2006.

Education World. (2000). *Teachers learn from looking at student work.* Accessed at www.educationworld.com/a_curr246.shtml on July 15, 2007.

Elmore, R. (2000). *Building a new structure for school leadership.* Report for the Albert Shanker Institute. Accessed at www. shankerinstitute.org/Downloads/building.pdf on February 3, 2008.

Epps, S., Ysseldyke, J., & McGue, M. (1984). Differentiating LD and non-LD students: "I know one when I see one." *Learning Disability Quarterly, 7,* 89–101.

Epstein, J. L., & Dauber, S. L. (1991). School programs and teacher practices of parent involvement in inner-city elementary and middle schools. *Elementary School Journal, 91,* 289–305.

Fletcher, J., Fuchs, L., Lyon, G., & Barnes, M. (2006). *Learning disabilities: From identification to intervention.* New York: Guilford Press.

Fletcher, J., Simos, P., Shaywitz, B., Shaywitz, S., Pugh, K., & Papanicolaou, A. (2000). *Neuroimaging, language, and reading: The interface of brain and environment.* Washington DC: Office of Bilingual Education and Minority Languages Affairs.

Foorman, B. R. (Ed.). (2003). Early developement and plasticity of neurophysiological processes involved in reading. *Preventing and remediating reading difficulties: Bringing science to scale* (pp. 3–21). Baltimore: York Press.

Fuchs, L., & Fuchs, D. (2003). Curriculum-based measurement: A best practice guide. *NASP Communique, 32*(2).

Fuchs, D., Fuchs, L., & Compton, D. (2003, December). *Responding to nonresponders: An experimental field trial of identification and intervention methods.* Paper presented at the National Research Center on Learning Disabilities Responsiveness-to-Intervention Symposium, Kansas City, MO.

Fuchs, L., Fuchs, D., & Hamlett, C. (1989a). Effects of alternative goal structures within curriculum-based measurement. *Exceptional Children, 55,* 429–438.

Fuchs, L., Fuchs, D., & Hamlett, C. (1989b). Monitoring reading growth using student recalls: Effects of two teacher feedback systems. *Journal of Educational Research, 83,* 103–111.

Fuchs, L., Fuchs, D., Hamlett, C., & Allinder, R. (1991). The contribution of skills analysis to curriculum-based measurement in spelling. *Exceptional Children, 57,* 443–453.

Fuchs, L., Fuchs, D., Hamlett, C., & Stecker, P. (1990). The role of skills analysis in curriculum-based measurement in math. *School Psychology Review, 19,* 6–22.

Gallegos, E. (2007). RtI changes concept of child find, aligns with goal of IDEA '04. *The Special Educator, 23*(1), 5.

Greeno, J. (1997). On claims that answer the wrong questions. *Educational Researcher, 26*(1), 5–17.

Gresham, F. (1991). Conceptualizing behavior disorders in terms of resistance to intervention. *School Psychology Review, 20,* 20–36.

Hanushek, E. (1992). The trade-off between child quantity and quality. *Journal of Political Economy, 100*(1), 84–117.

Hord, S. (1997). *Professional learning communities: Communities of continuous inquiry and improvement.* Austin, TX: Southwest Educational Development Laboratory.

Hunt, J. (1961). *Intelligence and experience.* New York: Ronald.

IDEA Reauthorization. (2004). *Joint explanatory statement of the committee of conference.* Accessed at www.cec.sped.org/AM/Template.cfm?Section=Search&template=/CM/HTMLDisplay.cfm&ContentID=7839 on April 8, 2008.

Individuals with Disabilities Education Improvement Act of 2004, Public Law 108-446, 20 *U.S. Code* 1400 (2004), et seq.

iSixSigma®. (2006). *Six sigma: What is six sigma?* Accessed at www.isixsigma.com/sixsigma/six_sigma.asp on February 3, 2008.

Jacobs, H. (1997). *Mapping the big picture: Integrating curriculum and assessment K–12.* Alexandria, VA: Association for Supervision and Curriculum Development.

Jensen, E. (1998). *Teaching with the brain in mind.* Alexandria, VA: Association for Supervision and Curriculum Development.

Lave, J., & Wenger, E. (1991). *Situated learning: Legitimate peripheral participation.* Cambridge, England: Cambridge University Press.

Leithwood, K., & Riehl, C. (2003, January). *What we know about successful school leadership.* Task Force on Developing Research in Educational Leadership. Research brief prepared for the American Educational Research Association by the Center for Educational Policy Analysis. New Brunswick, NJ: Rutgers University. Accessed at www.cepa.gse.rutgers.edu/What%20We%20Know%20_long_%202003.pdf on January 13, 2007.

Little, J., Gearhart, M., Curry, M., & Kafka, J. (2003). Looking at student work: For teacher learning, teacher community, and school reform. *Phi Delta Kappan, 85*(3), 229.

Local Accountability Professional Development Series. (2004). *Research base: A focus on essential standards.* Accessed at www.wested.org/pub/docs/616 on February 3, 2008.

Louis, K. S., & Kruse, S. D. (1995). *Professionalism and community: Perspectives on reforming urban schools.* Thousand Oaks, CA: Corwin Press.

MacIver, M., & Farley, E. (2003). *Bringing the district back in: The role of the central office in improving instruction and student*

achievement. Baltimore: Johns Hopkins University, Center for Research on the Education of Students Placed at Risk.

Mahoney, J. (1990). Do you have what it takes to be a super superintendent? *The Executive Educator, 12*(4), 26–28.

Marston, D., Fuchs, L. S., & Deno, S. L. (1986). Measuring pupil progress: A comparison of standardized achievement tests and curriculum-related measures. *Diagnostique, 11,* 71–90.

Marzano, R. (1998). *A new era of school reform: Going where the research takes us.* Aurora, CO: Mid-Continent Research for Education and Learning.

Marzano, R. (2003). *What works in schools: Translating research into action.* Alexandria, VA: Association for Supervision and Curriculum Development.

Maslow, A. (1970). *Motivation and personality* (2nd ed.). New York: Harper & Row.

McCracken, B. (2002, Fall). *Response to intervention: Policy considerations and implementation.* Alexandria, VA: National Association of State Directors of Special Education.

Meier, D. (2002). *In schools we trust: Creating communities of learning in an era of testing and standardization.* Boston: Beacon Press.

Mid-Continent Research for Education and Learning. (2003). *Sustaining school improvement: Data-driven decision making.* Aurora, CO: Author.

Moneta, G. B., & Csikszentmihalyi, M. (1996). The monitoring of optimal experience: A tool for psychiatric rehabilitation. *Journal of Personality, 64,* 275–310.

Nash, O. (1940). *The face is familiar: The selected verses of Ogden Nash.* Garden City, NY: Garden City Publishing.

National Center for Learning Disabilities. (2005). *Keep kids learning: A new model to identify students with learning disabilities before they fail.* Accessed at www.ncld.org/index.php?option=content&task=view&id=299 on March 28, 2006.

National Center on Student Progress Monitoring. (2007). *Common questions for progress monitoring.* Accessed at www.studentprogress.org/progresmon.asp#2 on February 3, 2008.

National Education Association Teaching and Learning Team. (2000, July). *Data-driven decision making and student achievement.* Washington, D.C.: National Education Association. Accessed at www.escholar.com/files/NEA-data_driven_decision.pdf on February 3, 2008.

National Institute of Child Health and Human Development. (2000). *Teaching children to read.* Report of the National Reading Panel. Washington, D.C.: U.S. Department of Health and Human Services.

National Reading Panel (2000). Report of the National Reading Panel: Teaching children to read. *Reports of the Subgroups.* Washington, DC: National Institute of Child Health and Human Development.

National Technical Assistance Center on Positive Behavioral Interventions and Supports. (2008). Program brochure. U.S. Office of Special Education Programs. Accessed at www.pbis.org/files/brochure.pdf on March 8, 2008.

No Child Left Behind Act of 2001, Public Law 107-110, 5, 115 Stat. 1427 (2002), et seq.

Northrup, J., & Gully, V. (2001). Some contributions of functional analysis to the assessments of behaviors associated with attention deficit hyperactivity disorder and the effects of stimulant medication. *School Psychology Review, 30,* 227–328.

O'Neill, J., & Conzemius, A. (2006). *The power of SMART goals: Using goals to improve student learning.* Bloomington, IN: Solution Tree.

Omrod, J. (1999). *Human learning* (3rd ed.). Upper Saddle River, NJ: Prentice Hall.

Papanicolaou, A., Simos, P., Breier, J., Fletcher, J., Foorman, B., Francis, D., Castillo, E., & Davis, R. (2003). Brain mechanisms for reading in children with and without dyslexia: A review of studies of normal development and plasticity. *Developmental Neuropsychology, 24*(2&3), 593–612.

Payne, R. (2003). *A framework for understanding poverty.* Highlands, TX: aha! Process, Inc.

Piaget, J. (1960). *The child's conception of the world.* London: Routledge.

President's Commission on Excellence in Special Education. (2002). *A new era: Revitalizing special education for children and their families.* Washington, D.C.: U.S. Department of Education.

Reschly, D. (2003, December). *What if LD identification changed to reflect research findings?* Paper presented at the National Research Center on Learning Disabilities Responsiveness-to-Intervention Symposium, Kansas City, MO.

Sanders, W. (1999, Fall). Teachers! Teachers! Teachers! *Blueprint Magazine, online edition.* Accessed at www.dlc.org/ndol_ci.cfm?contentid=1199&kaid=110&subid=135 on March 28, 2001.

Sanders, W., & Horn, P. (1994). The Tennessee Value-Added Assessment System (TVAAS): Mixed methodology in educational assessment. *Journal of Personnel Evaluation in Education, 8*(1), 299–311.

Sanders, W., & Rivers, J. (1996). *Cumulative and residual effects of teachers on future student academic achievement.* Knoxville, TN: University of Tennessee Value-Added Research and Assessment Center.

Scanlon, D. M., Vellutino, F. R., Small, S. G., Fanuele, D. P., & Sweeney, J. (2003, June). *The short and long term effects of different types of early literacy intervention on reading comprehension.* Paper presented at the annual conference of the Society for the Scientific Study of Reading, Boulder, CO.

Schmoker, M. (1996). *Results: The key to continuous school improvement.* Alexandria, VA: Association for Supervision and Curriculum Development.

Schmoker, M. (2006). *Results now: How we can achieve unprecedented improvements in teaching and learning.* Alexandria, VA: Association for Supervision and Curriculum Development.

Schunk, D. (2000). *Learning theories: An educational perspective* (3rd ed). Upper Saddle River, NJ: Prentice Hall.

Scruggs, T., & Mastropieri, M. (1992, Winter). Remembering the forgotten art of memory. *American Educator, 16*(4), 31–37.

Shinn, M. R. (Ed.). (1989). *Curriculum-based measurement: Assessing special children.* New York: Guilford Press.

Simos, P., Fletcher, J., Bergman, E., Breier, J., Foorman, B., Castillo, E., Davis, R., Fitzgerald, M., & Papanicolaou, A. (2002). Dyslexia-specific brain activation profile becomes normal following successful remedial training. *Neurology, 58*(8), 1139–1140.

Skinner, B. (1953). *Science and human behavior.* New York: The Free Press.

Snipes, J., Dolittle, F., & Herlihy, C. (2002). *Case studies of how urban school systems improve student achievement.* Accessed at www.mdrc.org/publications/47/full.pdf on March 18, 2008.

Sugai, G., & Horner, R. H. (2005). Schoolwide positive behavior supports: Achieving and sustaining effective learning environments for all students. In W. H. Heward (Ed.), *Focus on behavior analysis in education: Achievements, challenges, and opportunities* (pp. 90–102). Upper Saddle River, NJ: Pearson Prentice Hall.

Tilly, W. D. (2003, December). *How many tiers are needed for successful prevention and early intervention? Heartland Area Education Agency's evolution from four to three tiers.* Paper presented at the National Research Center on Learning Disabilities Responsiveness-to-Intervention Symposium, Kansas City, MO.

Tilly III, W. D., Reschly, D. J., & Grimes, J. P. (1999). Disability determination in problem-solving systems: Conceptual foundations and critical components. In D. J. Reschly, W. D. Tilly III, & J. P. Grimes (Eds.), *Special education in transition: Functional assessment and noncategorical programming* (pp. 285–321). Longmont, CO: Sopris West.

Togneri, W., & Anderson, S. (2003). *Beyond islands of excellence: What districts can do to improve instruction and achievement in all schools: A leadership brief.* Accessed at www.learningfirst.org/publications/districts on September 12, 2005.

Torgesen, J. K. (2000). Individual differences in response to early interventions in reading: The lingering problem of treatment resisters. *Learning Disabilities Research and Practice, 15*(1), 55–64.

Torgesen, J. K., Rose, E., Lindamood, P., Conway, T., & Garvan, C. (1999). Preventing reading failure in young children with phonological processing disabilities: Group and individual responses to instruction. *Journal of Educational Psychology, 91,* 579–594.

University of Connecticut. (2006). *Assessment primer: Curriculum mapping.* Accessed at web.uconn.edu/assessment/mapping1. htm on February 3, 2008.

Van Houten, R., & Hall, R. (2001). *The measurement of behavior: Behavior modification.* Austin, TX: PRO-ED.

Vellutino, F. R., Scanlon, D. M., Sipay, E. R., Small, S. G., Pratt, A., Chen, R. S., & Denckla, M. B. (1996). Cognitive profiles of difficult to remediate and readily remediated poor readers: Early intervention as a vehicle for distinguishing between cognitive and experiential deficits as basic causes of specific reading disability. *Journal of Educational Psychology, 88,* 601–638.

Vygotsky, L. S. (1978). *Mind and society: The development of higher mental processes.* Cambridge, MA: Harvard University Press.

Waters, T., Marzano, R., & McNulty, B. (2003). *Balanced leadership: What 30 years of research tells us about the effect of leadership on student achievement.* Aurora, CO: Mid-Continent Research for Education and Learning. Accessed at www. mcrel.org/PDF/LeadershipOrganizationDevelopment/ 5031RR_BalancedLeadership.pdf on February 3, 2008.

Whalen, S. (2005). Revisiting the problem of match: Contributions of flow theory to talent development. *Great Potential Press Talent Development IV,* 317–328.

Wright, J. (2005). *Curriculum-based measurement: A manual for teachers.* Accessed at www.jimwrightonline.com/pdfdocs/ cbaManual.pdf on March 15, 2008.

Electronic Resources

AIMSweb®
www.aimsweb.com

Florida Center for Reading Research
www.fcrr.org

Intervention Central
www.interventioncentral.org

The IRIS Center at Vanderbilt University
www.iris.peabody.vanderbilt.edu/rti/chalcycle.htm

Looking at Student Work
www.lasw.org

Maze reading (Maze-CBM)
www.aimsweb.com/measures/maze

National Association of School Psychologists, Response to Intervention References and Web Links
www.nasponline.org/advocacy/rtireference.pdf

National Center for Learning Disabilities
www.ncld.org

National Center on Student Progress Monitoring
www.studentprogress.org

Oral Reading Fluency, 90 Years of Measurement, Behavioral Research and Teaching
www.brtprojects.org/techreports/ORF_90Yrs_Intro_TechRpt33.pdf

Positive Behavioral Interventions and Supports
www.pbis.org

Put Reading First: The Research Building Blocks for Teaching Children to Read

www.nifl.gov/partnershipforreading/publications/reading_first1.html

Research Institute on Progress Monitoring

www.progressmonitoring.org

University of Minnesota (curriculum-based measurement research)

www.cehd.umn.edu/Pubs/ResearchWorks/CBM.html

The University of Texas at Austin (sample lesson plans and professional development)

www.texasreading.org

Make the Most of Your Professional Development Investment

Let Solution Tree schedule time for you and your staff with leading practitioners in the areas of:

- **Professional Learning Communities** with Richard DuFour, Robert Eaker, Rebecca DuFour, and associates
- **Effective Schools** with associates of Larry Lezotte
- **Assessment *for* Learning** with Rick Stiggins and associates
- **Crisis Management and Response** with Cheri Lovre
- **Classroom Management** with Lee Canter and associates
- **Discipline With Dignity** with Richard Curwin and Allen Mendler
- **PASSport to Success** (parental involvement) with Vickie Burt
- **Peacemakers** (violence prevention) with Jeremy Shapiro

Additional presentations are available in the following areas:

- Youth at Risk Issues
- Bullying Prevention/Teasing and Harassment
- Team Building and Collaborative Teams
- Data Collection and Analysis
- Embracing Diversity
- Literacy Development
- Motivating Techniques for Staff and Students

Solution Tree
555 North Morton Street
Bloomington, IN 47404

(812) 336-7700 • (800) 733-6786 (toll free) • FAX (812) 336-7790

email: info@solution-tree.com
www.solution-tree.com

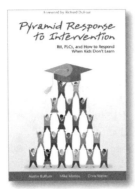